27.50

D0142080

The CULT
Experience

CONTRIBUTIONS TO THE STUDY OF RELIGION
Series Editor: Henry W. Bowden

The CULT Experience

ANDREW J. PAVLOS

CONTRIBUTIONS TO THE STUDY OF RELIGION, NUMBER 6

Greenwood Press
WESTPORT, CONNECTICUT
LONDON, ENGLAND

Library of Congress Cataloging in Publication Data

Pavlos, Andrew J.
    The cult experience.

    (Contributions to the study of religion,
ISSN 0196-7053 ; no. 6)
        Bibliography: p.
        Includes indexes.
        1.   Cults.   I.   Title.   II.   Series.
BP603.P38   291   81-13175
ISBN 0-313-23164-8 (lib. bdg.)   AACR2

Library of Congress Catalog Card Number: 81-13175
ISBN: 0-313-23164-8
ISSN: 0196-7053

First published in 1982

Greenwood Press
A division of Congressional Information Service, Inc.
88 Post Road West, Westport, Connecticut 06881

Printed in the United States of America

10 9 8 7 6 5 4 3 2 1

This book is dedicated to Thomas V. and
Anthony T. Pavlos and especially to Charlotte
Altizer Pavlos, whose enthusiasm for life and
interest in the extraordinary is infectious.

Contents

Series Foreword

New cults appear in every era when psychological uncertainty and sociopolitical upheaval cause people to question accepted values and seek new ones. In our own time a great number of religious groups with startlingly different beliefs and diverse lifestyles have attracted thousands of followers, particularly young people who reject the standards inherited from mainstream American society. Youth's search for new truth and higher values has led many to identify with cults, either domestic or imported, and this volume focuses primarily on that dynamic but volatile segment of today's religious population. Andrew J. Pavlos has been trained in the psychological and social branches of the behavioral sciences, and he uses these insights to discuss three basic aspects of the cult experience: conversion, commitment to, and identification with various units. Pavlos does not claim that his perspective adequately covers all aspects of these diverse phenomena. He reviews the content and theory of extant literature and finds that the subject does not lend itself to definitive treatment or a single answer. Instead, he has wisely chosen to provide an accurate, readable book for the general public, showing how his special fields provide insight.

Why do people join cults in the first place? Pavlos spends a great deal of time on conversion experiences and considers general models for this psychological transition. He does not indulge in sensationalism or let apparent trickery distract him from sober analysis of tangible factors. In discussing a convert's personal relationship with a particular cult, Pavlos suggests progressive steps that a prototypical individual has probably experienced. He focuses on the consequent personal attitude and what has led to such a receptive state of mind, especially the disappointment of failed social protest, and the positive charisma of cult leaders. Later chapters include a long look at such leaders as they exercise power and demand obedience from their followers.

How does the cult reshape individuals after conversion? The author concentrates here on the structural characteristics of group relations and reports interesting findings on the ways different cults enforce commitment among their adherents. We observe a large spectrum of groups, ranging from such large ones as the Unification Church and the Krishna Consciousness Society, to average ones like Synanon and People's Temple, to small communities represented by the Lake City organization and the Church of the True World. Amid this diversity of beliefs and practices we see common emphases on group pressure and similar enforcement techniques to keep members cooperative. Each in its own way follows methods to create viable group dynamics that demonstrate how ideas held within the circle are valid because they function well there.

What is the overall effect of cult membership on personal identity? After describing conversion and commitment, Pavlos turns at the end to a more evaluative form of analysis. In assessing the impact of the cult experience he considers ways in which cultists can become psychologically disabled. The author does not judge specific cults or leaders in detail but rather evaluates them in light of fundamental rules about social stability and personal mental health. He is particularly helpful in outlining the problems confronted by those who never capitulate to the new group. Those persons eventually leave the cult and experience many difficulties in adjusting to mainstream American culture again. In this section Pavlos also evaluates the questionable deprogramming assaults to which many former cultists have been subjected.

In light of his detached appraisal of cultic differences, the author also comments on the current status and future prospects of many groups studied here. In all, he has tackled hard questions about an intricate process that has many variables. His thoughtful findings provide both stimulating and enriching information about an aspect of religious behavior that we need to comprehend more fully.

Henry Bowden

Preface

The Cult Experience is an account of the emergence of religious cults in the times in which we live. One might assume that a period that has brought great scientific, technological, and social change would have also produced the social forces making it all but impossible for these new religions to surface. If we are to more fully understand cults, we must examine the new religious ferment and its effect on society. This book, therefore, tells how these new religions got started, how they have shot out of their historical roots into one of the most flamboyant expressions of religious plurality of our times, and how their self-styled prophets have proselytized young idealistic religious seekers.

Present-day messiahs and gurus have often been accused of exploiting young people, who were disillusioned and alienated from our major social institutions, seeking a new self-image and more positive identity. I trace the events that render these young identity seekers vulnerable to conversion and commitment to a cult religion and ideology. I discuss the precariously extralegal work of deprogrammers, who attempt to deconvert converts through methods labeled "reverse brainwashing" and "mind control." My focus then shifts to the aches and pains of readjustment to a postcult lifestyle for those who consider themselves fortunate enough to leave their cult identity behind.

The Cult Experience examines the current status of the new religions in the changing American religious scene and speculates on their future. Special emphasis is placed upon ways that have been proposed to stem the tide of religious cults in America.

My interest in religious cults began in the early 1970s, when I was more than curious about the apparent demise of politically oriented protest movements on college campuses, as the Vietnam War came to an end. A tumultuous period arose that saw young idealists turn away from political issues and search for spiritual reawakening. As representatives of this new period, these young idealists, who were not strangers to feelings of powerlessness, loneliness, and alienation from our educational and occupational systems, turned their backs on society and followed the calling of a new dream: the charismatic religious cult leader's messianic blueprint for a new age—the ultimate utopia.

In acknowledging those who made this book possible, I want to mention first of all the students enrolled in my Cult Movement course at George Williams College. They apparently were eupeptic enough to digest my lectures, which formed the core of the manuscript. Their critical comments have helped in shaping many of the ideas.

Lest I leave the reader with the view that this writing is mine alone, I should like to acknowledge Bill Gum, my editor, who was most helpful in editing the manuscript during its writing. Finally, I am especially grateful to my wife Charlotte Altizer Pavlos, who did the preliminary copy editing and the secretarial task of typing and retyping the manuscript; she was a constant source of encouragement and gave constructive criticisim. She managed somehow to squeeze in long hours of work and remain a warm friend and loving wife.

1

The New Religion and Cults: A Quest for a New Identity

What Is a Religious Cult?

"Cult" is a term elaborately illustrated and defined in textbooks on social movements and collective behavior. But what exactly do sociologists and social psychologists mean when they refer to a religious cult? In the most general sense, a religious cult usually involves a relatively small religious group whose beliefs, values, and practices are at variance with those of dominant or traditional forms of religion. On a more particular level, Hadley Cantril (1969), a social psychologist, defines a cult as "a deviant organized action, generally rather restricted and temporary, in which the individual zealously devotes himself to some leader or ideal" (p. 123). E. L. Quarantelli and Dennis Wenger (1973) describe a religious cult as "a diffuse group exhibiting inward innovative behavior that both differentiates and makes for conformity among group members and which is supported by religious beliefs and an ideology" (p. 384).

Although cultists have often been labeled by the media as deviant relative to members of more traditional religious groups, a cult is not normless. It has a normative structure and, usually, a well-established social organization. But this is often why its very existence tends to evoke negative reactions from the noncult community. A cult is an important reference group for its members.

That is, members identify with their cult and depend on it for social support and for a comparison and definition of what they construe as social and physical reality. Finally, cults develop religious and/-or political ideologies that provide a rationale for their beliefs and religious practices, as well as their very existence.

On a more pragmatic or popular level, journalists Carroll Stoner and Jo Anne Parke (1978) tell us that there are several criteria parents and their children can use to ascertain whether or not any one of the new religious movements is in fact a religious cult. They tell us how to recognize a cult:

1. Cults have living leaders and the cult's religious doctrine is based on the leader's revelations and ideology.
2. A cult's religious leader has absolute authority over his members.
3. Cults promise converts that through hard work and loyalty they can save humanity from sin and eventual destruction.
4. Cults require that members do "demeaning work" for the cause.
5. Cults promise everlasting salvation for faithful followers.
6. Converts must remove themselves from greater society – jobs, schools, families, and friends – and devote full-time effort to the cult and its leader.
7. Cults indoctrinate members through elaborate and extreme personality, attitude, belief, and behavioral change techniques.
8. Cults discourage critical thinking and suppress alternative views of social reality.
9. Cults create strong feelings of dependency on the group and demand absolute obedience to cult norms or standards for behavior.
10. Cults practice religious rituals or meditative techniques that are psychologically unwholesome to their members.

Cults have evoked such strong negative reactions from "popular writers" that many have claimed that brainwashing is used to change people's personalities (Conway and Siegelman, 1978; Stoner and Parke, 1978). Unfortunately, objective assessments of religious cults, as a means to understanding them, have been slow to emerge. According to J. Stillman Judah (1978), not all religious scholars or psychologists agree with popular writers that cults always have had unwholesome effects on their members. Judah claims that we need an objective investigation of both sides of this issue because writers seem to report only affidavits from parents who strongly object to their children's religious choice. Writers do not report that many parents do not feel that their children have experienced harmful personality and belief changes nor that they have been exploited by the cult or alienated from their family or school.

Some of the characteristics described by Stoner and Parke (1978) can also be found among traditional religions. However, the differences between cults and traditional religious groups are more pronounced than the similarities. Conventionally oriented religious groups typically do not isolate people from the outside world. Nor do they demand total loyalty to their group or absolute obedience to their religious leaders. In other words, traditional religious groups generally accept society's social standards. They do not expose their members to rigorous resocialization processes. Nor do they ask their followers to accept doctrines that reject society in order to build a new utopia. Cults rely on faithful followers to generate a sustained membership. To this point, psychologist George W. Swope (1980) interviewed over 125 young people who had dropped out of a wide variety of cults. He concluded that a cult's membership consists of the following kinds of people:

1. *Idealists* who want to know God better.
2. The *innocent* who naively believe that a cult messiah is God's divine representative.
3. *Inquisitive* young college or high school dropouts who suffer from severe and demoralizing family and personal problems.
4. *Independent* young people who run away from home seeking freedom from parental restrictions and authority.
5. *Identity seekers* having trouble believing in themselves.
6. *Insecure* youth looking for new experiences and a clarification of their own identity.

C. Eric Lincoln and Lawrence Mamiya (1980) have proposed that there exists three general characteristics of most cults necessary to convert people totally to a cult lifestyle: 1. *Communicative isolation*, when cult members are told not to disclose the "esoteric dogma" of their cult to "outsiders." 2. *Social isolation*, when the cult members reduce extracult contacts and live in an autocratic cult group. 3. *Physical isolation*, when cultists are required to live in communes and are forbidden to leave without the cult's permission.

A religious cult is a religious group whose leader formulates the group's dogma and isolates the members from others who would normally support their original beliefs. Members become dependent on the cult for the satisfaction of their needs. The cult leader gains absolute control over the behavior of members through an elaborate system of rewards and punishments. Finally, cults are identified as deviant religious groups whose members are generally labeled by the noncult community as religious "kooks" or "crazies" (Swope, 1980).

Religious cults have often been regarded by social scientists as social movements, which are organized attempts on a relatively large scale to change society (or resist change), generally through noninstitutionalized means (Toch, 1965). Most social movements go about seeking change by focusing on the problems of inequality or disfranchisement. The civil rights movement is an example of a social movement. These movements generally develop in such a way that it is not always clear whether or not they accept preestablished social norms or legal or social sanctions. The sociologist Herbert Blumer (1969), believes that cults are a special kind of social movement, because just like any other form of social movement, they emerge from social unrest. Some writers believe that Christianity originated as a social movement, attempting to convert people to what was then characterized as a different set of religious beliefs. Anthony Wallace (1956) suggests that all of the established religions of the world began as social movements. These religious social movements, just as present-day cults, sought to change people's living conditions by conversion to the doctrine of the religious group. When a religious movement organizes its members to bring them back into the fold, its activities take on the character of a revitalization movement. A revitalization movement is a deliberate and organized attempt to construct what is perceived to be a more satisfying social order. Like revitalization movements, religious cults do not necessarily limit their activities to saving the individual, they reach out in an attempt to transform society into what they believe is a perfect social order.

Ernst Troeltsch (1931), a student of Max Weber, described how traditional religion differs from sects in terms of a *church-sect dichotomy*. For example, Troeltsch noted that churches are part of a society's established institutions and they attract their membership from certain social strata. Established church leaders and political leaders can be at odds over various issues; however, established religious leaders recognize the political establishment. They usually are willing to compromise their beliefs with existing secular interests by adopting the goals of the greater society. Established religion has a theology that has been debated and formulated over a long time: Christianity, Hinduism, Buddhism, Judaism, and Islam are the major established world religions. Sects, on the other hand, are newer, smaller, and, above all, less formally organized. They arise among those who are alienated from established religion and do not generally wish affiliative ties with mainstream religion. Sects generally have their origin as a schism from an established church. Leadership is charged to the minister or priest who has been selected by others and has usually undergone special training to reach this position. The leaders are considered specialists who can elaborate the doctrine of the church. Sects have a converted membership. They stress direct revelations and personal religious experiences rather than rigorous formal training and established theology.

Robert N. Bellah (1967) uses the term *civil religion* to describe our national faiths that support our political system. Civil religion is united by a commonly shared belief in God, generally derived from the major traditional religions and they invoke God to bless political gatherings. Even politicians use civil religion as a way of establishing credibility for their office.

Why a Psychological Perspective on Cults?

Few social phenomena have intrigued social scientists as much as the behavior of groups who are determined to solve their personal problems through organized, deviant religious action. A study of religious cults is indeed an interesting and contemporary topic. Although new religious movements can be investigated from a variety of scientific perspectives, it is the psychological view, based on social influence processes, that has a special fascination for me.

A psychological perspective on new religions in general and cults in particular differs substantially from sociological and anthropological perspectives. Apart from differences in theories and research methods, sociologists generally tend to focus on different problems than psychologists (Blank, 1978). By and large, American sociologists study what they consider to be unconventional culture groups in toto. These groups often have had their origin abroad and have appeared on the American scene. For example, sociologist William M. Kephart (1978) examined a few select sect groups in terms of their diversity and their attempts to eliminate or replace most of the basic alternatives to traditional family and community living by religious-based settings (e.g., the Amish, the Shakers, and the Mormons). Kephart focused on the social structure of each sect and attempted to ascertain the long-lasting influence of the sect on the family and its members. He was less concerned with the behavior of individual sect members, except for that of the leader. Kephart examined leadership by focusing on the political, economic, and religious factors that influenced the leader's style or format. It is generally in this sense that sociologists seek to understand the subcultural similarity and diversity of people's social behaviors in group interaction: the central unit of concern is the group. This perspective is in sharp contrast to that of psychologists who focus on differences in personality and study the social patterns of influence that stem from close interaction with others; they do not focus on the group per se.

When anthropologists study religious groups in different cultural settings, they view culture as the total way of life of a given group of people. That is, they examine the culture's ways of serving the biological and social needs of a society as a whole. For example, anthropologists study the culture's science, religion, mythology, and its forms of social control. The anthropological approach to religious cults can be illustrated by some observations on cargo cults by Peter M. Worley (1959).

The underlying belief of cargo cults is that a deceased cult leader, a hero, the devil, or the spirit of dead ancestors will return in a truck, ship, or airplane loaded with a cargo of goods that has been made in heaven for the survival of the natives. However, this cargo has somehow been diverted by the white man. The cult leader claims that there will be a return of the cargo to its rightful owners, followed by an era of plenty. The leader promises the people that they will be liberated from alien domination and that there will be a new social order based on justice and peace.

Worley writes that cargo cults have appeared in many different parts of the world and occasionally they have been so well organized and "fanatically" persistent that people have abandoned their property, making this the reason why these religious beliefs have been considered to be dangerous to the welfare of numerous societies.

Worley's observation of cargo cults raises several questions concerning our assumptions about human behavior. The Ghost Dance religion, practiced by the Indians of the Great Plains in the late 19th century, is yet another religious cult studied by anthropologists. These people suffered greatly at the hands of white intruders. Whites slaughtered their buffalo and brought disease that killed off many Indians. Because of this, many Indians turned to the peyote cult as an escape from their depressed conditions. They did extensive proselytizing in an effort to flee from the harshness of their world (Barber, 1941).

Anthropologists focus on the general characteristics of a particular culture; psychologists seek explanations that account for the wide diversity of individual differences in religious beliefs in any cultural setting. But when we shift to the psychological perspective, we must also identify what forces mobilize the particular individual cult member into organized or collective action when the situation seems to call for such action. Sociologists tell us that some sort of organizational structure, formal or informal, seems necessary for people to act in concert. Hence, the merit of a sociological perspective on religion is that it concentrates on the organizational aspects of human behavior in groups, allowing us to go beyond the limitations of individual psychology, which focuses more on the person (Glock and Stark, 1965).

Only when we realize how the individual member is tied to the cult group can we begin to understand how the cult group can influence the individual's behavior. If we realize this, it becomes obvious that a cultist's behavior cannot be accounted for solely by appealing to individual predispositions or to the cult group members alone. However, if we extrapolate from folk wisdom, we must beware of certain pitfalls. Everyday experience, or common sense assumptions, suffers from incompleteness and our biases. In contrast, a comprehensive study of religious behavior tends to focus on the group as well as the individual members of the group. This allows us to develop an understanding of the relative stability of religious behavior over time and under different circumstances.

Does this mean that it is hopeless for psychologists to investigate or even describe complex social behavior or indeed behavior of members of a religious cult? Not so, because when psychologists focus on the individual's social behavior, as long as they do not lose sight of the structural characteristics of cult groups, as a whole, insight into complex social behavior can be gained (Wilson and Schafer, 1978). However, when we do a psychological analysis of religious cults, we must understand the basic assumptions on which the science is based. According to psychologists, people have emotional and cognitive needs that they ordinarily attempt to satisfy by social means. One's immediate social surroundings are important, and one's special motives, attitudes, and belief systems tend to influence one's social behavior. Hence, it is not too difficult to demonstrate how personal factors as well as social factors alter our behavior in any given social context or setting.

Although the science of psychology has not yet reached a point where complex social phenomena can be fully explained, it takes only a few variations on well-established psychological principles to account for the social influence processes that seem to operate on the cult-group level (McGuire, 1967; Pepitone, 1976). Rather than focus only on the general societal conditions said to give rise to groups, social psychologists also focus on the characteristics of a person's belief system, especially the strong beliefs that direct the person toward religious forms of behavior.

The now classical research of Muzafer Sherif (1936) and Solomon Asch (1956) on the emergence of group norms or standards for conformity is relevant for a psychological analysis of how the individual's behavior is determined by the actions of the group. The individual is confronted with an ambiguous situation. Past values and beliefs are highly likely to operate. However, strong group pressure is shown to influence the individual's judgments in the direction of the group's estimate of physical and social reality even though the judgments of those present may in fact be erroneous.

What Asch's and Sherif's research tells us is that the critical beliefs and judgments of a person are due in part to the erroneous judgments of others. The degree to which this is true depends on whether or not the person believes that the group possesses the power to bring about conformity or compliance, not on the objective reality of the stimuli being judged. This is true in spite of criticism that Sherif's and Asch's research paradigms really do not show a "true group effect" (their subjects did not interact as a group). Nevertheless, Sherif's and Asch's experiments give us important insights into the fundamental processes of group-oriented behavior. But we still need studies that link such research to real-world situations (Campbell, 1957; Carlsmith et al., 1976).

The formation of a cult's beliefs and values emerge when cult leaders attempt to define reality and reveal this to their members. When there is an apparent lack of knowledge of some fact, the group tends to fill the gap. Because cult members' beliefs and values can best be satisfied within a group setting, they tend to reach a certain consensus about the goals of the group and indeed about the group's definition of social reality (Festinger, 1954).

The key, then, to a cult group's influence is the vulnerability of members to social influence. Most young idealists who join cults are vulnerable because once they have become members some of the most sophisticated techniques of thought control often take hold. Only the cult's reality is considered valid. The cult group becomes an ever demanding circle of social pressure to bring about uniformity of behavior and beliefs. The shrinking distinction between private and public behavior in cults suggests that the preponderant direction of the cult's prescriptions for behaving is made obvious to its members. They come to accept these prescriptions because to do otherwise would destroy the group's plans for a perfect social order.

Traditional religious beliefs as the determinant of behavior is short lived in the cult setting because the personal forces that drove youth to cults are a sense of alienation from Protestant, Catholic, and Jewish mainstream religions. These religious doctrines are perceived by the new religious seekers as decadent as they search for an identity that has its origin in what they label the strivings for a more meaningful human existence. The stress on individualism or personal happiness is a pervasive theme in the new religious movements. There is a search for new social roles as a means of transforming society into a utopia.

Even though it may seem like a tour de force to derive a series of generalizations about cult-related behavior from the application of psychological principles, many statements about the behavior of cultists can be stated in terms of psychological generalizations and still on balance not be imprecise. The basic idea is that a variation on psychological principles, as a way of evaluating cults, may not be too premature at this time if indeed we compromise between some empirically derived social psychological principles and some real-world observations.

Besides examining religious cults from basically a psychological point of view, I will also incorporate topics of historical and sociological importance. I will also strenuously depict notions of religious doctrine, especially the strong and pervasive spirit of the new religions. Then, it can be seen that this is a book about what has been labeled "the cult movement" and it is only peripherally concerned with traditional or orthodox religion. Basically I will try to explain why today's youth is especially vulnerable to the influence of the new groups and messiahs and their seemingly bizarre cult theology. I will also try to show that as a secular society sometimes we tend to underestimate the great power of messianic religious leaders and their persuasive techniques. What the reader must remember is that these leaders believe in what they are doing because they claim to have a divine calling. This divine calling of the prophet sometimes starts with a narrow vision and may expand to an apocalyptic dream by predicting that the cult leader will take over, and even if the cult is ridiculed or maligned, the obsession does not stop there. The cult leaders' dreams for utopia are legitimized by their divine calling. Cult followers are isolated and secluded from the outside world with little or no way to check the messiah's delusion or dream for utopia. Hence, from the perspective of social science, cults represent a group of deviant religious followers. This is why we should consider what social and personal conditions seem to surround a particular cult movement. We also need to know what promise of redemption or salvation or threat of disaster could tempt people to take up a cult lifestyle in the first place. Without much exception, followers of cults, other than cults like Krishna Consciousness Society, have devotees who do not seem to embrace an entirely new religious ethic or dogma. This is why they can take part in the cult's ritual that they do not fully understand but still they are able to achieve self-validating experiences. This is so because these adherents of the new religious movements seem to share a common search for self-fulfillment and what they construe as success by not drawing upon given traditions and by not embracing mainstream religious ideals, but by faithfully practicing the religious ritual set out for them by their cult authority figure — the cult leader.

The following six chapters will provide illustrations of several kinds of cults. By using these examples, I will trace the steps from a cult conversion to a cult identity. In this way, I will attempt to show how vestiges of what has been labeled extremism are preserved in the cult. Although a belief in a cult's religious ideology, dogma, or its practices does not, as a rule, really improve the cultist's condition, it seemingly ameliorates for the moment the travails of disillusionment and despair, and, as such, it permits a special kind of survival under otherwise desperate circumstances. While all of this is going on, many of the messiahs and gurus, or Gods in a Rolls Royce, are getting richer and stronger despite the mounting criticism from the media and outraged parents.

Because cultists are likely to come to accept a religious ideology that differs from the beliefs they held before becoming a cult devotee, I will consider the dramatic process of cult conversion. This is especially relevant in recent years when cults like Reverend Moon's Unification Church and Hare Krishna systematically go out and recruit large numbers of converts. Hence, unlike many traditional religious efforts, the cult advocates engage in extensive proselytizing. I will take stock of the conversion and commitment processes that often result in cult members accepting an apocalyptic vision that offers them an escape from the seeming harshness of a world that they have been taught to believe is filled with corruption and sin. I will describe a series of steps through which converts pass before they reach a point of total cult conversion: where religious seekers internalize the cult's beliefs and spend great time, energy, and money on behalf of their cult leader and his enterprise. I will also describe how cult leaders use their special charismatic talents to persuade their converts to accept and become totally committed to a cult lifestyle. Deprogramming will be discussed along with the current status of cults. Finally, I will trace the historical roots of the cult movement in my search for a cult prototype.

The Origin of the Current Cult Movement

The 1960s witnessed two striking phenomena on the American scene: the emergence of protest movements directed against the political establishment and new religious movements directed against the religious establishment. Increasingly, the young moved away from the old credo that if you study hard in school and later take on expected responsibilities of family and work you will be rewarded by the good life. They turned instead to an active pursuit of self-fulfillment and the search for a new and more positive self-identity.

Today there has been a shift away from the politically oriented protest movements of the 1960s. Many youths are now preparing themselves for careers in the advanced industrial society that their counterparts in the 1960s so vehemently criticized. Yet an increasing number of young people feel isolated from our complex society and are lonely. They have few close ties or satisfying relationships. An even greater proportion of young people are being attracted to the new religions than was the case in the 1960s (Needleman and Baker, 1978). Nearly every university campus and large community has its share of resident gurus or messiahs. Are many of today's young people turning to these new religious movements in ever increasing numbers because they seek a genuine spiritual and moral change or are there other, less obvious and perhaps less admirable reasons for their doing so? Because we are unsure what to believe or what conclusions to draw, we must be cautious in generalizing about the new religious movements. Nevertheless, because these religious preferences seem so different from traditional religion, we may conclude that the new religions, in general, and cults, in particular, represent a break from more established religion. We want to understand what it is about society that makes it possible or even likely for the emergence of a cult religion or any religion that splinters off from traditional dogma.

By the 1970s many Americans had left the churches of their childhood and turned to secular pursuits or to the new religion. Because of this, we seem to be losing our hold on our most important ethical and religious values. Many young people no longer trust our most basic social institutions as a source of direction. Few young people these days believe that they retain personal control and responsibility over the direction of their lives (Fabry, 1968; Lefcourt, 1973, 1976). This apparent conflict in ethical and religious values is why some young people have dramatically turned to the new religious movements for solutions to their personal problems. This is why religious cults like Reverend Sun Myung Moon's Unification Church, Guru Maharaj Ji's Divine Light Mission, Swami Prabhupada's Hare Krishna, and Ron Hubbard's Church of Scientology have met with alarming success throughout the United States.

Since cults are admittedly out of the mainstream of American life, the first question that this book on cults should address itself to seems simple and straightforward: Why are so many young people joining cults? The problem with attempting an absolute answer to this question is that there is genrally no one acceptable answer. However, if we sidestep this question, we still need to know what exactly the consequences are for the individual who joins a religious cult.

I will attempt answers to both these questions, but first, it should be noted that the belief in cult religion and its ideology is not new. What makes the current growth of cults noteworthy, with their appeal toward fostering what is described as a "new self-authenticating experience," is that it is taking place in an age of science and rapid social change.

As a phenomenon, many religious cults are part of a currently widespread interest in such practices as exorcism, witchcraft, voodooism, mysticism, and astrology. An interest in the preeminence of such beliefs is deeply rooted; these beliefs are not just the product of the 20th century. Rather, they are what has been described as "powerful life-enhancing realities" (Bird, 1978). Throughout history, beliefs in spirits or forces in the universe beyond human control have exerted a powerful influence on the way people charted their lives.

Religious dogma has often been a barrier to rational thinking and free and open inquiry. At the present time, the dogma of cults are more irrational and absolutist than that of more established religion. Paradoxically, it is often to the cult religion that disillusioned and estranged young people can turn in time of trouble and despair, reaching out for a new and more positive identity and for meaning in their lives. What social, psychological, and spiritual factors can motivate such a profound and pervasive need? The social conditions surrounding this phenomenon as well as the psychological makeup of cult devotees and their cult leaders, who have drawn the blueprint for what they consider the new and perfect society, must be taken into account.

The recent interest in the cult phenomenon originated in part from the trend of the past two decades toward antimaterialism and the search for self-identity and self-fulfillment. We still need to ask: What best characterizes what has been labeled the current cult movement? This is difficult to answer because there is little agreement among contributors to the sociological or psychological literature, with the exception of an occasional attempt to demonstrate that cult members are deviant religious seekers or that there are conditions in contemporary society that give rise to messiahs or gurus who seem ready and able to exploit widespread dissatisfaction. Many cult leaders are convinced that they do in fact have special godlike characteristics; they profess to offer a special kind of redemption or salvation not readily provided by traditional religion. On a more pragmatic level, these new religious groups offer a supportive community for young people during a time when they are searching for what Erik Erikson (1968) calls a "new identity." According to Erikson, traditional religion plays a central role in the development of many American adolescents. For many, adolescence is a period of high commitment to their parents' religion. But as the youths mature they struggle to develop their own belief systems, often quite different from those of their parents. Erikson believes that these adolescents are searching for religious beliefs as part of their quest for identity and that this search for self-definition can create an identity crisis.

Although traditional religion is important to many adolescents, a relatively small, but highly visible, number of American youth have sought nontraditional religious beliefs. It is also well known that it is older adolescents and youths who are attracted to cults (Doress and Porter, 1978). Younger children, just as elders, do not often seek out cults. Some writers argue that older adolescents, beginning to move away from their parent's beliefs, have not yet committed themselves to a philosophy of life that they can claim as their own (Doress and Porter, 1978; Roof, 1978). Hence, for some young people the religious cult represents a spiritual search. For still others who join cults, this may be a way of seeking attention, adventure, and a "new experience" (Doress and Porter, 1978). Young people who seek love and acceptance, wanting at the same time to contribute to the betterment of society, can find cult involvement one way of extricating themselves from all that seems wrong with the outside world. Also, some young people claim that they have found a "pipeline to God" through the teachings of a messiah or a guru, although evidence suggests that a great price may be paid for this seemingly tranquil and blissful existence. Indeed some cults can reduce their followers to a kind of "robotlike functioning" (Singer, 1979).

There is a great difference in the kinds of people who joined cults a few decades ago and those religious seekers that have joined cults in recent years. During the 1940s and early 1950s, the people who joined cults were not seeking to change the world through self-fulfillment nor did they believe that they could do something for themselves and for society at the same time (Judah, 1978). Today's cultists are different from their predecessors. Most of them are white, come from middle-class homes; have some college education; are twenty to thirty years of age, and have been at least peripherally involved in religious activities a great part of their lives. Most importantly, they claim that they are seeking more meaningful lives, are disillusioned, and are alienated from society as a whole. Furthermore, they are searching for self-fulfillment and a way to save the world from what they consider corruption and sin (Stoner and Parke, 1978).

In order to comprehend the nature of religious cults, we must first look at the special social conditions that foster them and the kinds of people likely to accept a new religious belief system. We should consider what conditions shape and sustain a religious belief system when immediate social pressures and outside support for these beliefs are absent. Most members of a given cult are in fair agreement with one another about the nature of the cult group's way of perceiving the world, especially when special norms or standards emerge and are used to judge what is construed as physical and social reality. This is why the social atmosphere of cults is not generally such that one could expect to find the same definition of reality as one is likely to find in more ordinary situations. At best, a different kind of truth emerges in the cult. Seeking what is construed as the truth, fact, or reality is characteristic of most people. This is no less important for religious seekers who end up joining a religious cult than for anyone else.

Differences of opinion exist among the members of any particular cult, since social reality means different things to different people. When one examines some of the reasons why people join cults and then cling tenaciously to their beliefs, it becomes obvious that any useful explanation must take into account the many different ways in which people derive their conceptions of social reality. This means that we must examine what makes cult devotees think, feel, and act the way they do. Above all we should ask: What are the special conditions found in a cult that profoundly alter the way its members perceive the world? When we ask this, we must realize that it is only in recent years that we have begun to understand why people choose to become absorbed in religious cult groups. Modern psychology has learned much about how people go about seeking answers to complex questions, especially in small groups where at first disparity and some disagreement exists among members. People do not act the same way in all situations (Bem and Allen, 1974). Each situation, including interaction within a cult, that holds what is considered by noncultists as extreme or polarized beliefs, affects the behavior of members in different ways. Different conditions in each situation may cause different behavior by the same person. Thus people who claim to have witnessed a religious cult leader produce a miraculous faith cure may in so doing deny the truth of their senses, which they would be unlikely to do in other circumstances. People do not always act independently of the group. One's view of the world can sometimes be based on a false group consensus. That is, a group-based distortion can enter into a situation and influence one's judgments when one is bent on seeking absolute truths (Asch, 1956). In such cases, values arise from people's expectations, producing a tendency to accept what is expected in the situation (Goffman, 1971). It is this tendency that makes the situation credible. A group's values and norms satisfy its members' expectations. It can also be argued conversely that a situation meets the group's expectations because it satisfies the members' values and norms.

How well does social science research explain complex social behavior that is tied to group action? A fair amount of recent psychological investigation has been aimed at seeking to understand the conditions that determine whether or not a person is likely to form lasting group relationships and whether in doing so, that person undergoes belief and value changes. To analyze the cult movement, it is necessary to sort out the social forces that lend support to group unity and coherence. Certain beliefs and values are central to the basic premises of any religious group, whereas others are only peripheral or even incidental to the maintenance of the group.

Our present knowledge of the new religions, like that for many other complex social science phenomena, is not all that we should like it to be. Nonetheless, the cult movement evokes much special interest and curiosity. Some form of unorthodox religion can be found in almost every part of the country, although the form and its degree of unorthodoxy of the religious practice has varied widely. For example, the snake-handling cults of the Appalachian region of the United States employ a ceremony in which members handle poisonous snakes as part of a ritual used to express members' faith that God will protect them from impending danger. The snake-handling is preceded by long hours of testimony by members about being saved by the Holy Spirit, fervent prayer, and ecstatic dancing that often produces complete exhaustion in many members. Next, boxes of water moccasins, copperheads, and rattlesnakes are displayed. Members pick up the snakes and twine them around their bodies. This religious ritual is practiced in West Virginia (where it is still legal) and Kentucky, Tennessee, and Virginia, although illegal there. Many people are attracted to these services (Gerrard, 1971).

The snake-handling practice appears strange; however, the tragedy of Jonestown, Guyana, where more than 900 people died in horrifying mass suicide-murder, under the direction of Reverend Jim Jones, indicates the degree of fanaticism some cults can display (Krause, 1978; Lincoln and Mamiya, 1980). By comparison, the revivalism preached by evangelists such as Billy Graham, who seeks to recover people from what he believes are their wayward and sinful ways through "born-again" conversion, is relatively "harmless." Billy Graham and his born-again crusade is obviously different from the snake-handling cults of Appalachia or the People's Temple in the relative absence of extreme and fanatic behavior.

Do certain people within any community have a greater likelihood of joining a religious cult than do others? Because questions like this have been raised, some psychologists have looked for a cult-prone personality. However, the best evidence we have suggests that we are not able to predict complex social behavior like that of religious seekers from measures of personality traits (Mischel, 1968, 1977). This is so because it is highly unlikely that cult-related behavior is the product of personality characteristics alone. The decision to join a religious movement depends on a variety of social and personal factors (Goleman, 1978).

The kinds of situations people encounter affect their tendencies toward certain kinds of actions and not other behaviors (Endler and Magnusson, 1976; Penner, 1978). Because of the wide spectrum of individual differences in personal attributes and styles of social interaction, it can be argued that the behavior of religious seekers must involve special motives and religious beliefs that are based on the kinds of beliefs and behaviors found in any religious cult setting. For example, imagine someone who believes that most people are living in conditions of sin and corruption. This person also believes that the only hope for salvation and redemption is to follow a religious leader with a rigid, unwavering code of ethics. Such a person may be attracted to a religious cult. Even in such a case we still need to know more about the individual's values and beliefs in order to understand why the individual has concluded that the only salvation is through a religious commitment. In order to gain any degree of understanding of the person's religious choice we would have to take into account the strong situational and environmental factors that operate. K. S. Bowers (1973) maintains that to some degree one determines the situations into which one enters. People tend not to select situations at random but those that seem to be consonant with their religious and ethical values and beliefs. This implies that an individual is highly unlikely to seek out a nontraditional religious group when that person's religious beliefs and values better fit a traditional ideology or conventional religion.

The interaction of peoples' beliefs systems and situational factors is viewed within the framework of a psychological theory of human behavior that has now grown to a position of prominence (Jones et al., 1979). For instance, we now believe that in serving the interests and motives of group members cults such as the Unification Church tend to have a great and lasting influence on their members. In such cases, the particular cult is more than a collection of individual cult members. For example, suppose that a cult leader seeks to justify his group's existence. An important question to ask is whether members of the cult can be motivated to view their membership to be important enough to satisfy their long- and short-range interpersonal goals. If this is the case, will members protect their religious group in case of threat to its existence because they are protecting their way of life? This question is difficult to answer. However, we know that some religious beliefs are sufficiently motivating or inspiring in themselves that tremendous effort can be forthcoming in order to save the cult from outside forces (Krause, 1978; Lincoln and Mamiya, 1980).

When considering who joins cults, we should realize that although most people seem able to cope somehow with the demands of our modern bureaucratic social order, there are others who are not. Most people who feel abandoned or disillusioned by the more conventional aspects of society remain dissatisfied yet they do not seek freedom from society's constraints by joining religious or politically oriented groups. But still others do join some sort of group in an effort to ameliorate their feelings of personal frustration and despair. In fact, Hans Toch (1965) tells us that countless people have been swept into social movements, like cults, only to later become unhappy victims of a "fanatic and distorted vision" because they had been caught up in the ideology or the religious dogma of autocratic leaders. Fortunately most people seem to avoid this kind of entrapment.

If cults are to recruit large numbers of people successfully, they must promise greater security and happines than is available in more traditional settings. They must appeal to those who feel unfilfilled and exploited by society. The United States is an especially fertile breeding ground for religious cults partly because of the changes in lifestyles during the 1960s, partly because of the religious freedom in our society, and especially because more established institutions, such as the family and the school, have been hard put to provide the emotional security and intimate social support and love sought by many people in our complex society (Bronfenbrenner, 1970).

A key element in the current cult movement is the promotion of social change in society along with the promise of greater satisfaction for the individual cult member. Hence a major goal of the cult movement is the forging of a different self-identity and a more positive self-concept for its members. There is also a promise (generally unkept) of movement toward self-determination and self-respect, eminently claimed to underscore the basic charting of the cult member's life. This is especially important to people emerging from accumulated deprivations and injustices to seek some form of corrective measure.

Among today's young people there is a trend toward seeking a sense of meaningfulness and self-enhancement. In recent years many have sought to develop an image of themselves and of society that allows them to live more meaningful and creative lives. Some are attempting to do this in a religious cult setting (Yankelovich, 1974).

2

Becoming a Cultist: Conversion to a Cult

How Conversion Takes Place

Except from psychologists of religion, conversion to cults has received little attention from psychologists. Empirical data concerning conversion to cults are relatively absent from the literature (Paloutzian et al., 1978). Nevertheless, the study of religious behavior and beliefs from a psychological perspective remains an intriguing topic because religious experiences is an intense and universal characteristic despite its wide variations in theological and ideological interpretations of the phenomenological experience of religion (Dittes, 1969). Can social psychologists describe and explain the process of religious conversion or is this a topic beyond a social psychological purview? On a more general level, can psychological and sociological descriptions of religious cults handle issues connected with a cult identity as this takes place through one's religious experience? This is an important question because we need to explain the powerful influence of a religious group on its members, especially when most religious cults are intentionally designed to manipulate certain desired ends. We also need to know whether or not conversion to a cult's theology and belief system can be described as an individual process or whether there are more general social factors involved that must be taken into account. In other words, is conversion the result of conscious striving or does it happen to individuals without their desiring it or even against their intentions or will? Following this line of thought, Alland (1962) describes how the manipulation of sensory factors induced or stimulated trancelike states and mystical experiences in members of unconventional groups under conditions of what he describes as *sensory deprivation*. Alland observed that when these individuals are subjected to sensory deprivation their body movements are almost completely eliminated, they had little sensory imput, and they were confronted by a situation producing great fear and anxiety. Then, in full view of the cult minister, they were told that they should report any feelings of personal salvation and the presence of God. As the hand of the charismatic minister was placed on the converts' head, they reported visual and auditory hallucinations; that they heard God speak and felt the strong presence of God. Alland claims that all this can take place independent of group pressure or influence.

Peter Suedfeld (1975) summarized research on sensory deprivation and concluded that people are likely to find that mild sensory deprivation can be pleasant, whereas extreme forms of sensory deprivation can be unpleasant. Under extreme sensory deprivation people often show decreased intellectual functioning and mood shifts and even visual and auditory hallucinations.

Because sensory deprivation can diminish an individual's ability to resist attitude and belief changes, it is relevant for an understanding of cult conversion. The stress that may occur during periods of sensory deprivation makes some individuals especially sensitive to social influence. The psychological effects of sensory deprivation, as it is produced in a cult setting, can have extraordinary outcomes. Some religious converts have emerged from the new religions, and especially cults, with emotional disturbances and even delusions. Some report that they were unable to perform more or less routine tasks or to concentrate on anything other than their private religious experience.

As is the case with most complex behaviors that shake our conception of human nature, a variety of causative factors must be sought so that we can produce an explanation for conversion to a religious cult belief system and practice. In line with this reasoning,

John P. Kildahl (1965) suggests that vulnerability to sensory deprivation, "enlightened suggestibility," and "hypnotizability" are typical characteristics of persons who experience a sudden conversion to an extreme religious belief system and ideology. Sigmund Freud (1950) claimed that unconscious motives are at work in religious conversion: a hatred of one's father, a fear of verbalizing this fear, and a fear of one's father's taking revenge are propitiated in an acceptance of a religious leader's beliefs. Leon Salzman (1966) tells us that sudden converts are extremely dependent on strong, omnipotent figures and that they exhibit an exaggerated, irrational intensity of religious belief, accompanied by a crusading zeal.

If all this is true, how can it be determined what type of person, under different situations or conditions, is most likely to be converted to a religious cult? William James (1902) felt that psychologically immature individuals are the ones most likely to undergo a conversion to an unorthodox religious group: those who are introverted and pessimistic with a negative outlook on the world, one that is brooding and steeped in despair. In partial support of this view, recent studies show that revivalistically oriented individuals, who vary in age from the teens to late adulthood, join nontraditional religious groups when they are depressed, lonely, confused, and when their life seems meaningless (Conway and Siegelman, 1978; Singer, 1979). But suppose that people who possess unconventional religious beliefs and values have not yet concluded that membership in a religious cult can improve their prospects for a better life, what then can be said about the likelihood that such individuals will become members of a religious cult? To put the question another way, what makes people seek out other people who share similar unconventional religious beliefs? In answering this question, it seems only logical that if a religous cult is to become attractive it must promise personal growth and salvation and it must put forth a belief in a more perfect social order before potential converts are likely to consider joining. But are these the necessary and sufficient conditions to cause most people to seek out membership in a cult religion? Perhaps not. This is why I will consider other factors. When I have done this, I will attempt to ascertain whether or not it can be predicted that individuals who are approached by members of a cult are likely to be converted unless they already have the kind of beliefs that are on the surface at least consonant with those of the cult group.

At first glance, one can conclude that most religious cults group members hold beliefs that denounce the values of the greater society. They preach an imminent and disastrous end of human suffering and pain and believe in a utopian ideal. These are the sort of religious beliefs that demand that cult members remove themselves from their friends and family and relinquish any real connection to personal property and educational goals. This is so because most cults stress an apocalyptic future that calls for the rejection of the present world for being evil and abysmally corrupt. Because the religious cult is future-oriented, there is little need for personal-property or old ties.

If people hold strong unconventional religious beliefs, feel rejected by society, believe they are unworthy, and have low self-esteem, one might expect that they would seek out those who are accepting and caring. And one would guess that these people's attraction to a cult is likely to increase just as long as the cult does not appear to be insincere or to confuse or contradict their strong religious beliefs. And, if such people encounter cult members who promise a new life, the likelihood of joining the cult obviously increases. However, once these people have joined a cult group, they may not be willing to make the necessary sacrifices required to maintain membership. Some individuals who are not initially interested in the promise of a new life, or in salvation, may join a cult because they are at least intrigued by the prospect.

Does this mean that there is a sequential arrangement of events that describes the process by which individuals are systematically selected in and out of a cult? Are persons considered likely prospects by religious leaders for cult recruitment because they are available and their religious beliefs and values are sufficiently intense to produce the necessary conversion to the cult group's ideology? If this is so, how can we determine when a particular person has in any deep sense taken on a cult group identity or perspective? The most obvious evidence that people have done so is their own declaration that they in fact have been converted. This may take the form of a claim of rebirth or regeneration or what is more generally labeled a *religious conversion* (Glock and Stark, 1965).

Verbal claims of conversion cannot always be trusted so we must observe what the convert does as well as what the person says. John Lofland (1966) differentiates between *verbal converts* and *total converts: Total converts'* words match their deeds. This is not necessarily the case with *verbal converts;* they may not practice what they preach.

Conversion can be sudden or it can be gradual. A gradual conversion may take place over several months or years (Scobie, 1973). However, it must entail an emerging strong commitment to religious values and beliefs and it must encompass evidence of behavioral commitment to the religious group's dogma and its practices (Scroggs and Douglas, 1967). This is why a member is pressured by the group to act on his or her religious values and beliefs. Duane A. Windemiller (1960) finds striking similarities between brainwashing, as practiced by the Chinese Communists, and techniques applied in religious conversion. In both cases, there is a drastic change in one's belief system and mode of thinking. This is brought about by strong group pressure entailing interrogation, training in "clear thinking," and public confession of one's errors or sins. While all this takes place and while physical exhaustion and "hypnoticlike" suggestions are applied, new labels are introduced for one's behavior and beliefs. When such conditions are present, people show intense self-criticism, doubt, fear, and guilt. When in a religious context, potential converts reach a high level of physiological arousal and they begin to talk freely about their past sins, the cult group and its leader guides the convert toward a "recognition of the absolute truth."

The religious cult member must learn to adopt the peculiar reasoning processes and beliefs known as a *cult-group perspective.* Particular stress is placed on "bad thoughts." Often cult members, just as prisoners of war, are required to express these negative thoughts spontaneously before the group (Lifton, 1961). This activity supposedly moves individuals to a point where they experience powerful emotional arousal, which emerges from intense personal, political, and religious feelings. Perhaps the most important result of being converted to a religious cult is the internalization of the group's religious values and beliefs; that is, the converts experience the group's values as their own (Doress and Porter, 1978).

In practice, however, all these possible combinations of psychological and religious factors are not always found. Such conditions may operate only when the potential convert has been made vulnerable to strong pressure to accept the cult's beliefs. In many cases, people who eventually commit themselves to a cult may do so more for the social support and the high degree of intimacy that they find within the cult's relatively small circle of ready-made friends. They may join a cult because of the intimate relationships that are found and not because of their religious beliefs.

Conversion can be regarded as both a personal and a group product. It does not always necessarily involve the chain of causality or events suggested by many current writers who hypothesize that only personal or only religious factors operate to cause intense changes in one's religious beliefs and activity. However, psychologists have identified certain determinants for peoples' social behavior, especially changes in behavior that take place in unconventional groups (Zimbardo et al., 1977). In such settings, according to cognitive dissonance theory, people's inconsistent beliefs arouse unpleasant psychological states, directing their behavior toward producing relative consistency between their beliefs and their actions. Most importantly, people in their private and public lives are said to seek consistency over inconsistency between their beliefs and their behavior. This implies that when people find themselves through choice, involved in or committed to an unconventional group whose beliefs and practices are at first somewhat at variance with their views, there is a tendency to change in the direction of the group because it would be even move inconsistent to do otherwise (Wicklund and Brehm, 1976). This strongly suggests that people do not have to agree with others' religious beliefs or practices completely; but as long as they remain in the cult they are highly likely to change in the direction of the group's beliefs and practices.

Conversion to a cult faith certainly is not all that common. It requires a special kind of commitment to an "absolute truth" that calls for surrender of all one's energies to the cause. According to John Lofland and Rodney Stark (1965), *total conversion* to a cult's dogma takes place when people: (a) experience enduring and acutely felt tensions (b) within a religious problem-solving context (c) that combine and produce a self-definition of that of the religious seeker (d) wherein potential converts encounter a deep religious feeling or a turning point in their lives; (e) then the potential converts form (or already have) an affective personal bond with one or more of the cult's converts, (f) this takes place under conditions where extracult attachments are relatively absent or at best neutralized, and, finally, (g) if people are to become total converts, they have to be expolsed to intensive interaction with faithful members of the cult.

Although the temporal nature of Lofland and Stark's model for conversion may vary from one cult to another, cults like the Unification Church can be considered typical because they ideally describe how people are attracted to and eventually become faithful and committed cult members.

The Lofland-Stark model suggests that many people drown their personal problems in a cult-group setting. This is why young idealists often are sought-after sources of strength for cult group leaders; they tend to conform to the social pressures of their peers and they are often responsive to authority figures. Such young people are likely to have a strong desire to be accepted as part of the group, especially when they forego former social ties. Young people who come to the cult find those that they interact with sources to validate their own sense of self-worth. When they do this they can avoid, or even escape from a seemingly threatening life; nevertheless, when their past social ties are cut off, they are often in trouble.

The Unification Church

One of the fastest growing cults in the United States in the past quarter century is the Unification Church of Reverend Sun Myung Moon. Who is Reverend Moon? Moon was born in 1918 in North Pyongan Province in what later was to become North Korea. He founded the Unification Church in Korea in 1954. Several years earlier, as a youth, Moon had experienced a "mountain-top vision" of Jesus Christ that changed his lifestyle. He claims that he was instructed by Jesus to carry out the work that Jesus had himself failed to complete while here on earth. In the late 1950s, Moon extended his movement to Japan and then to the United States, where he told his followers that man's fall in the Garden of Eden was due to more than the result of sin and adultery. According to Moon, Eve had sex with Satan and thereby corrupted the whole human race. Jesus, who Moon claims was not God, came to start a new and sinless humanity. He was supposed to have children through marriage to a virgin; however, according to Moon, Jesus failed his sacred assignment. In effect, Jesus only accomplished *spiritual salvation,* leaving *physical salvation* undone. According to Moon, when Jesus failed his divine mission he was thrown out of the Trinity. Then God searched for a new savior and after centuries found Moon.

Moon developed a cult religion consisting of a strange potpourri of Christianity, Taoism, and Buddhism. According to Moon's *Divine Principles,* if he blesses the marriage of cult members, this will restore them to the status of God's Kingdom. In effect, they are absolved of original sin through a *pikarume* or blood-cleansing process accomplished by begetting children from a "pure woman"; of course, with Moon's approval. In the end, Moon claims, he will save all humanity because God's Kingdom will be reestablished with the divine Moon as the absolute spiritual ruler and savior of mankind. And, according to Reverend Moon, America has a special role in God's plan and a special spiritual destiny (Sontag, 1977). Moon's major goal is a global crusade to expel from the world what he considers are the implied evils of communism. Moon believes that communism is the embodiment of the Devil here on earth. Moon has made obedience to his cult rules absolute. He has raised his members eschatological expectations to a high pitch. These beliefs are expressed by members of Moon's cult when they "hang out" at airports and around college campuses in an attempt to attract young converts. Thomas Robbins and his associates (1976) argue that the Unification Church represents an attempt to resacralize what Moon considers to be the disintegrating moral and political order.

Moon thinks that the United States is in grave danger of losing its status as "God's Promised Land." He believes that an imminent collapse of democratic society will take place because there is an abandonment of our traditional stress on *moral absolutism* (or the need to delay personal gratification) in favor of a consumer ethic or what Moon labels *moral relativism.* Moon feels that traditional American religion, instead of concentrating on a doctrine of spiritual life, has been compromising its moral stand on worldwide communism. He believes that moral absolutism has come under attack as permissive child-rearing practices became the dominant theme of our families.

Moon's followers believe that permissiveness has led to the increase in extramarital sex and divorce and that this in turn has led to the deterioration of the traditional American family. Moon claims that the Unification Church and global communism will have an "apocalyptic showdown" in which Moon, as head of God's Kingdom, will win out. The Unification Church, he claims, will reestablish universal moral and religious principles. This is why members of the Unification Church expend great effort to affirm Reverend Moon's attempt to save the United States and South Korea from China's Communist influence. This is also why the Unification Church gave early support to United States involvement in the war in Vietnam on the grounds that this was part of God's plan to attack worldwide communism (Robbins et al., 1976).

Where do members of Reverend Moon's Unification Church come from? Who are these "smiling and seemingly polite and euphoric Moonies?" For the most part, they are disillusioned young people whose initial feelings of alienation, despair, and isolation from the greater society are set aside to seek group consensus and social support for their unconventional religious beliefs (Cohen, 1975).

Philip Zimbardo and associates (1977) claim that the individual Moonie cult member is made to feel the group's power when social reinforcement is given out in terms of praise, smiles, acceptance, love, and the like. There is a call for conformity to a stringent group norm. Feelings of guilt and shame are engendered in those who show any form of deviant behavior or disagreement with

Moon's religious teachings or the group consensus expressing the need to save humanity. So it is that past commitments of "premies" are left behind. The Moonies create anxiety and engender apprehension over group acceptance. Zimbardo tells us that all converts are urged to meet the rigid social standards set by the Moonies. A dependent atmosphere is created where childlike obedience is fostered in converts. All those present at the initial conversion rites appear to be attractive, happy, and at times even euphoric. The vitality of the group is obvious.

The goals of the Unification Church seem admirable — love is the cure for all evil — a panacea for all that is wrong with the world. Then comes mind control with all of its esoteric trappings. Finally, commitment to the Unification Church's goals is often accompanied by what has been labeled a *group-shared messianic delusion.* But these are only a few of the things that influence the potential convert: all the principles of radical belief and attitude change are brought to bear on the situation (Zimbardo et al., 1977).

Frederick Bird (1978), a professor of religion and sociology, tells us that cults, such as the Unification Church, the Divine Light Mission, Hare Krishna, and Scientology, base their religious practices upon praxis rather than upon abstract religious dogma. That is, members of these religious cults practice stereotyped or habitual activities or rituals, such as initiation rites, meditation, and spiritual healing, to develop a sense of self-worth for their members. This is why religious rituals are important, and they are practiced by the cult's faithful members. To this end cult leaders employ repetitive, stylized ritual in order to communicate their belief to cult members and to guide them through what is proclaimed sacred. The use of ritual is expected to bring cult members a special kind of self-transcending and self-transforming experience much like that experienced in unconventional therapy groups. Silva Mind Control uses therapeutic ritual to train people to function as psychics. Meditation rites are used by Hare Krishna, the Divine Light Mission, and Transcendental Meditation.

Many other religious cults employ what psychologists call "total environment," in an attempt to bring about radical change in the values and attitudes of potential converts. But, contrary to what many observers claim, a weekend workshop alone does not lead to the conversion of most participants. Actually, only a small percentage of people who attend these workshops join a cult and maintain membership for a relatively long time. J. Stillman Judah (1978) claims that only about 10 percent of those who attend the Unification Church workshops are ever totally converted to its ranks.

One reason why many people join religious cults is that their parents' religion was not what they wanted, so they sought something different. A frequently observed characteristic of many young people who join cults is that they have changed their religious faith several times (Cohen, 1975). In varying degrees, they seem to suffer from alienation and a lack of identification with their culture and its more traditional religious values. After becoming converted to their new cult religion, these cultists claim that they no longer feel confused or ambivalent about their religious values and beliefs (Robbins et al., 1976).

Some former female members of Hare Krishna and the Unification Church movement say that they left because of the inequality of the sexes, especially former members of Hare Krishna, where traditional Hindu culture and religious teachings give males the dominant position. The Unification Church not only demands at least three years of celibacy before marriage, it then arranges the partners' marriage in a truly "Oriental fashion," where the male is dominant and must answer to the Moonie leaders for the couples' behavior. From observations such as these, Emily Culpepper (1978) has concluded that the new religious movements, such as the Hare Krishna and the Unification Church, offer female followers what she calls a *pseudo newness.* According to Culpepper, there is little reason to believe that the role of females within these movements will change from their traditional-patriarchal-nuclear family orientation. She tells us that even the religious principles preached are antifemale.

The example of the Moonies summarizes the portrait of the desperately estranged lives of many cultists. But why does the presence of others inhibit defining the situation differently? Converts must support the cause unconditionally because this is what *total commitment* demands. Without the close association with those already committed, transformation to a cult identity is unlikely to develop. On the other hand, once a religious movement takes hold, in this era of widespread electronic mass media, young people become more accessible. For example, one of the most impressive mass media blurbs is mention that life can be more fulfilling, as long as the young person publicly proclaims an interest in being born again. Many young cultists are seeking the coming of a New Age — a spiritual reawakening amcng tens of thousands of young people. Indeed, one is lead to believe that new gods are emerging from the ashes of antiquity to solve all of today's problems.

Cults and Their Relationship to Growth Groups

I have discussed how people become converted to a cult dogma and ideology. In this section, I am especially concerned with how the "group movement" is related to the "cult movement."

During the past twenty years, the number of people who have sought membership in groups oriented toward developing personal growth through closer relationships with other people has increased enormously. Under the rubric of T-groups, encounter groups, or sensitivity training, growth centers in the United States offer opportunities to join for relatively short or extended periods. Often special arrangements have been designed to promote an understanding of people who come from diverse social backgrounds, or who have nonconventional lifestyles, or seek self-understanding and group acceptance (Back et al., 1973). The groups that have emerged have special meaning for their members and are effective in changing their members' attitudes and behaviors.

One example of a growth group is est (Erhard Seminar Training). Mark Brewer (1975), in a highly critical analysis, claims that est employs the "fundamentals of brainwashing" and trappings of the language and practice of Eastern meditative religions, along with what he describes as "slick salesmanlike appeals to Westerners." Brewer suggests that the main thrust of this "therapy" is to tear people down, making them realize their worthlessness and undesirable lifestyle and then to attempt to rebuild their confidence and self-esteem, attributing any success to est.

Brewer asserts that the training is authoritative. Trainees are required to sit on uncomfortable chairs for hours. They then are required to reveal their innermost feelings as they are insulted by the group. After nearly eight hours of coaching, repetition, and meditation-directed instruction, most trainees are on the floor sobbing, groaning, and claiming that they are totally converted to est. These sobbing and groaning people are reminiscent of those at revival meetings who claim that they have been saved or born again.

The recent upsurge of groups has been attributed to many factors. For example, a strong reaction to the seemingly impersonal character of most forms of urban living and the increasing need for close relationships, even though they are sometimes somewhat temporary at best, have been used to explain the sudden increase in the belief that relatively small, organized group movements can yield deeper satisfaction than can ordinary, superficial day-to-day interaction in work groups and school communities (Back et al., 1973). Growth groups have attracted leading psychologists and psychiatrists. In some cases, for example est, these groups have attracted participants by their seemingly sudden solutions to complex human problems. Still other programs offer the group member a self-styled guru who professes to have the answers to people's complex personal, spiritual, and social problems.

What are these groups all about? The *sine qua non* of the encounter or the sensitivity group is the opportunity for self-assessment and objective self-awareness under what they claim are optimal conditions. However, the price can be conformity to the group's norms for self-disclosure. All too frequently some participants are made anxious about their acceptance. But, on the more positive side, some see a refreshing trend in the interest in Eastern philosophies such as yoga and Zen Buddhism, where meditation and altered states of consciousness are achieved without the use of drugs. The claim is that meditation can produce what is labeled a "natural high."

What accounts for this prodigious heterogeneity of group emphasis in so many different types of social settings? After all, people from the earliest times have formed groups for the purpose of survival or for the purpose of meeting the basic forms of social interaction. What does all this have to do with the "cult movement"? An understanding of growth groups can help to increase our understanding of how and why people join any type of group. Also, the best evidence suggests that with certain kinds of commitment to group norms or standards, people can change their beliefs and their behaviors in a positive or a negative way, depending on the particular group setting and its standards for behavior.

There is one important difference between growth groups and religious cult groups: people in growth groups, unlike those in cults, may never again or seldom again see those with whom they have interacted (Lieberman et al., 1973). Nevertheless, both cult groups and growth groups specify the conditions under which membership and social interaction take place. In both cases group membership entails personal benefits (rewards) and sacrifices (costs). Inspired by the potential for self-discovery, a group's members receive from others valuable information about how they are perceived; each group member is expected in turn to offer valuable feedback to others (Festinger, 1954). According to S. Duval and Robert A. Wicklund's (1972) objective self-awareness theory, people increase their self-awareness as a result of feedback from others. When people focus upon their own behavior, the information gleaned may tell them a great deal about the impact of their behavior on others. This is so particularly in those situations where people are uncertain about their own feelings. It would seem that through this process of self-perception people come to assess the consequences of their behavior on others (Kleinke, 1978).

All kinds of groups have the potential to change people. Growth group training and cult group interaction produce great change in their members' beliefs and behavior.

But there is still the question: Why do people join unconventional groups, such as cult groups, in their search for self-fulfillment? Unfortunately, data on this matter do not allow a precise answer to the question. It would seem that although we do not know for sure the many reasons for the apparent attraction of both the "growth movement" and the "cult movement," the fact remains that countless people, who on the surface may seem reasonably successful, seek added warmth, intimacy, and mutual support from people through close small-group interaction.

Cults and Their Relationship to Social Protest Movements

The attraction of certain contemporary religious cults to young people may have its roots in the social protest movements of the

1960s. Among the most important goals (ideals) of most social movements that emerged during the 1960s were the equipping of people to function better in a modern bureaucratic society; preparing young people for the responsibility of independent thinking; encouraging the growth of self-acceptance; and making sure that all people had an equal opportunity for education and employment regardless of race, sex, or socioeconomic class background.

The historian Theodore Roszak (1969) claims that during the 1960s there was a discernible consciousness among young people that he labels the *counterculture*. It entailed profound dislike for advanced technology and the commercial and educational enterprises that supported and proliferated technological society. Roszak asserts that education was used to mold youth to the needs of what he called a *baroque bureaucracy*, where democratic ideals became a matter of sensing the public opinion polls. At this time, high social status was available only to the affluent. This social condition left many young people with feelings of alienation and despair. Roszak, who agreed with Herbert Marcuse's (1964) *One-Dimensional Man*, maintains that young people became unhappy with bureaucratic demands.

As social movements spread during the 1960s, they attracted new members and supporters. It was during this time that most of the new religions emerged. These movements often took the form of crusades. Some evidence suggests that shortly after the mid-1960s, and up to the early 1970s, young people turned increasingly away from political issues, becoming involved in religious activities supposedly to bring about social change but mostly to seek greater self-fulfillment. Often this meant drastic changes in young people's patterns of personal and social interaction. This took place apparently through a conversion to the "new dogma of religious pluralism" so firmly embedded in our religious history (Yankelovich, 1974). At the peak of this era of political unrest, some youths turned to the new religions where people were not asked to nod their heads in response to decision makers. Young people who sought self-fulfillment were the first to turn to exotic religious experiences. Their basic premise was a belief in the goodness of human nature that came to influence their perception of society's future. They rejected the idea that economic well-being was the indispensable source of freedom and dignity for the individual. They derided their elder's identification of hard work and education as the road to self-fulfillment and success. They belittled what they perceived as bureaucratic harshness of everyday life and sought some measure of autonomy within the context of the new religions. As a result, they professed religious beliefs that flouted those of mainstream religion and indeed society as a whole. This is why, even today, much of the public hostility toward the modern cult movement is one of opposition to the cults' nontraditional beliefs and practices. Young cultists feel bitter over this lack of acceptance; they are disheartened by what they claim is rampant bias toward their cult membership (Doress and Porter, 1978).

Previously I stated that conversion to a cult religion is necessary (if not sufficient) for great personality and belief change to take place along cult-related lines. Commitment and conversion to a cult ideology prevents individuals from seeing themselves as other than followers who act at the behest of their cult leader. Once a person is converted, the individual is compelled to "keep the faith." The more unconventional the group's beliefs and behavior, the greater is the necessity to foster social controls for what is considered appropriate behavior. Barry McLaughlin (1969) suggests that "keeping the faith" implies that cult members need to protect their belief system from outside influence. Hence as cults emerged during the 1960s and 1970s, they needed to make their beliefs and values public in order to show what kinds of dissatisfactions they had and the kind of social changes they were seeking. As was the case with most protest movements in the 1960s and 1970s, religious cults blamed the social establishment as the villian.

Even if the cult ideology contrasts with what seems more reasonable to the individual at the time, and more socially desirable for many other people, if the goals of the cult are to become a reality, the group must seek power and use it generally through persuasion and coercion. And if a cult movement is committed to violence or revolutionary tactics as a means of achieving social change, this indeed is a likelihood. A cult group must have relatively clear-cut goals and it must promote satisfaction for its members. Often this is done through crusades and rallies; at other times the cult's members gather to reestablish their faith in the goals of their group through daily religious ritual and communal living.

Contemporary cults are different from most politically oriented protest groups of the 1960s in that they generally seek guidance from supernatural sources and they search for salvation, preaching transformation of society into what they consider a better life for its members. Cults have a strong belief that their prophecies will finally be fulfilled. There is the claim that cult members will be protected from the evils of society, whereas nonbelievers will perish along with society's evil and corruption. This is why cults are hideouts for religious seekers who are sensitive to the fact that they are not accepted by the more conventional aspects of society, whom they have counterlabeled as sinners and disbelievers (Freedman and Doob, 1968; Guten, 1978; Lofland, 1966).

The Impact of Social Pressure on Conversion

Psychologists interested in group-based deviancy believe that people's immediate social surroundings are important determinants of nonnormative or deviant behavior. The behavior of people in groups affects how they define their feelings, attitudes, behavior, and, in general, how they come to make sense out of their world (Festinger, 1954). Because of the ever present group effect, people take the easy way out when faced with strong social pressure: They tend to compare themselves with similar others. Whether people view themselves as religious seekers or not depends partly on how religious they believe they are in comparison with similar others. The behavior of other people provides important insights about oneself. That is, when one obtains information gleaned from those who hold similar beliefs and values, one comes to learn something significant about oneself. Research on the social comparison processes shows clearly that when individuals make more or less favorable comparisons with similar others, their self-esteem tends to increase, binding them closer to their social comparison group. On the other hand, when individuals compare themselves with dissimilar others, this is unlikely to occur (Morse and Gergen, 1970).

I now turn to some research that demonstrates the impact of people's reference groups on their attitudes and behaviors. Later, I will attempt more directly to show the relationship of some recent research to the understanding of the pervasiveness of cult group influence on individual members.

Phillip Brickman (1964) had Harvard undergraduates complete two questionnaires, one dealing with the students' own feelings toward the values of authority, sensuality, equality, and the manipulation of people and the other measuring the students' perceptions of how the same values operated at home and at Harvard. Then, just after the students returned from their Christmas vacation, they once again completed the questionnaire dealing with their own feelings toward these values. The major prediction tested was whether or not the students' second ratings would change toward their perceived Harvard norm or toward their perceived home norm. The results of Brickman's research clearly show that there is a strong tendency to maintain one's newly found beliefs even to the extent of becoming more firmly convinced that one is correct and one's family is wrong in their perceptions of the world.

Brickman's research shows that the values and beliefs of university students are influenced when they come home during Christmas and then return after vacation to their college environment. Students are members of one reference group in college and still another at home. While at college, students actively seek to share their beliefs and values. Under these conditions, the college student, much like the religious group member, is virtually compelled to participate in the group and as such he comes to share the values of his community. Often, when the students return from college to their reference group at home, even for a short time, people at home perceive and react to the student in terms of the college reference group. In this case, the student seems compelled to defend the college norms through taking the role of the typical liberal student. This tends to produce even greater commitment to the college norms than existed prior to coming home from college.

Brickman's findings are instructive for what they reveal about the impact of a reference group on the influence of students' beliefs. That is, Brickman's students' values shifted significantly in the direction of their perceived norm at college. In addition, those who spent the most time at home during Christmas vacation were most likely to change toward the Harvard norm.

Brickman's research shows that a person's reference groups can contribute greatly to how one views the world. The same kind of influence operates when considering the social influence processes found in a cult group setting. The acceptance of a cult group norm is a form of legitimating the members' reactions to the group and to outside criticism, especially when the members meet criticism from their noncult community. When there is opposition to the cult group norm, the conversion processes are strengthened. This is true as long as the factors that caused the conversion in the first place are similar to those that support continuance of faith in the cult's view of the world. This protects and correspondingly shields the convert from other views of social reality. So it is observed, then, that a strategy for protecting a particular view of the world is unwittingly a set of beliefs that are maintained in the face of opposition. This strategy works as long as the individual can reduce the cognitive contradiction from the outside world and still hold on to his or her religious convictions.

Hans Toch (1965) tells us that the common set of beliefs, values, and ideology of social movements (including cults) tend toward the extreme; yet members are usually highly committed to the group's cause. Perhaps this helps explain why when proponents of religious cults are met by strong opposition from their "outside community" they defend their beliefs even more strongly. Harold H. Kelley (1952) even suggests that one's reference groups can serve as a social standard for the individual's judgment of other groups. Recent research shows that one's out-groups are evaluated in an extremely negative way, especially when one's views are polarized (Linville and Jones, 1980).

Then, once again, why are people attracted to the new religious cults? Observations from everyday life, as well as some empirical evidence, suggest a common-sense answer: people prefer others whom they believe similar to themselves in beliefs and values and some people perceive religious cults as sharing their beliefs and values (Byrne, 1971). If people who convert to religious cults were truly objective, they might have considered alternatives that others perceive as rational and more practical. This is why the new religions are perceived as too utopian. Most people seeking religious truths believe that there surely must be more realistic ways to seek change or a new self-definition or identity than by joining a cult.

Present-day cults, with their esoteric beliefs and practices, encourage people to join and see God's truth for themselves firsthand rather than derive it from the scriptures or the seemingly platitudinious sermons heard in traditional churches. When the cult message is presented, certain people seem to be ready for conversion: they possess the religiously oriented beliefs and behavior Eric Hoffer (1951) labels *true believers*. Hoffer tells us that these true believers are people with little self-confidence who move from one group to another seeking affirmation and hope, searching for the cult and sometimes the occult where simple and appealing answers to complex questions can be found in spiritualism or faith-healing. If a conversion does take place, the convert is more than likely to become subservient to his or her newly found beliefs and values. True believers claim to have seen the light and that delusion and torment belongs to their past (Dohrman, 1958).

Charisma, Messiahs, Gurus, and Prophets

A "divine calling" from a cult leader can gather a group of faithful religious followers who expect to be lead to the promised land. An apocalyptic vision can have the consequence that even reason seems to pale before the awesome power of the cult leader. There is the impulse to obey, to turn over responsibility for one's decisions to the leader. Such dedication is possible because there is an absence of a rational challenging of the rules, often considered sacred. Instead, there is a sense of reverence and loyalty to the cult leader and to the cult group. To be loyal to the cause is, in effect, to endow the cult leader with *charisma*; this binds converts to the realities of the situation. Hence, to respond irrationally is not to yield to one's ability to do critical thinking.

Just who are charismatic leaders? About eighty years ago, Max Weber (1963) described charismatic leaders as people who are set apart from ordinary people and are treated as though endowed with supernatural, superhuman, or, at least, exceptional powers or qualities. Overwhelmed by the leader's qualities, ordinary people follow without question or criticism. This is true whether charisma is immediately or only rather slowly recognized by followers. However, charismatic leadership must be linked to the situation to be understood fully. For example, one is unlikely to accept a leader, even though he lays claim to a divine or utopian promise, unless what the leader has to say makes sense or is more or less consonant with one's belief system and values in the first place.

Charismatic religious leaders possess certain information; they have an important message to be imparted and they think the best way to do this is to gain the attention of a large number of people not yet aware of this "divine calling." In a sense, charismatic leaders have what psychologists label *credibility*, the perception by others that they posses expertise and trustworthiness. But they have more: they have the ability to manipulate others through what has been described as a "divine inspiration" (Cohen, 1975). They challenge people with their evangelistic or messianic messages. Even the name of the religious cult leader (e.g., David "Moses" Berg) or the cult group (e.g., People's Temple or Children of God) may lead some people to assume that the leader or the cult's members have special personality traits or "divine characteristics" in common. It soon becomes clear who is the leader and who are the followers. The cult leader is the person who has charisma, a messianic prophet; the followers are those who have been "born again" within the cult setting; they are Hoffer's true believers who have found their cult messiah.

So it appears that cult leaders emerge in connection with and in cooperation with their devoted followers. People are likely to accept a charismatic cult leader when they perceive that his or her beliefs and values are similar to their own. Factors, such as the leader's authority, status, social power, and past record of successful leadership set the stage for the cult leader's style. In the case of the charismatic religious leader, his or her leadership style in most cases has emerged long before a relatively large number of followers have joined the cult (Gibb, 1969; Hollander and Julina, 1969; Stogdill, 1974).

Reliable historical evidence shows that cult leadership, under the direction of a charismatic, is most likely to become fanatic or extreme when cult members face a crisis or threat to their well-being (Lincoln and Mamiya, 1980; Stern, 1975). In such cases, loyalty to the leader, even when the leader's behavior is inconsistent or seemingly pathological, remains steadfast when the cult leader is able to confront his or her followers and to convince them of his or her integrity and the worth of the goals of the cult. While at the height of this crisis, the charismatic cult leader can emerge with relatively high credibility. This is especially likely to take place in leadership situations that Eric Hoffer (1951) labels charismatic and where followers are *true believers.* These are people who seem to have little self-confidence, hoping somehow to discover a new meaning for life and to obtain solutions to their immediate personal problems in a cult setting. Hoffer tells us that true believers are likely to move from one group to another, always dissatisfied and in search of meaning in their lives until they finally encounter a group that offers utopian solutions to the world's problems.

Eventually, some cult leaders become sanctified; to their cult group they are in effect an incarnation of God (Weber, 1963). When this occurs, the cult group may demonstrate loyalty to their leader, even to the extent of violent collective behavior. This seems, in retrospect, to be what occurred in the case of the mass suicide-murder among Jim Jones' followers in the jungle of Guyana. It is important to consider less extreme incidents that precede such violent action. That is, when the preconditions are there, a "fanatic" cult leader, such as Jim Jones, can summon absolute obedience to his will because the group is predisposed to follow him. This is especially true when the followers are true believers who are cut off from all other views of reality.

The cult leader obtains oppressive control over people who are alienated from the "normal" power of the community. Such followers learn to distrust all but members of their own religious cult. Even new converts pledge loyalty to the cult leader's religious beliefs and ideology. Cult leaders can easily take advantage of followers. His or her mission can be understood to imply that he or she seems to believe that the end justifies the means. In view of the powerful tendency of young people to follow charismatic leaders, how do so many avoid being drawn into the vortex of cult forces? This question begs an answer I have not yet fully explored, nevertheless, I will examine the intricacies of this process in subsequent chapters.

Tentative Conclusions about Cults

So far I have attempted to give some understanding of the many social and personal determinants that give rise to the formation and maintenance of religious cults. I have stressed that as conditions in our complex society continue to depersonalize young people, we might expect to observe a proliferation of new religions. We might also expect that our understanding of the conditions that foster their formation will increase as more researchers and writers focus their efforts and attention upon this problem. Meanwhile, there are some generalizations that can safely be made about the rise of the current cult movement. First, cults are partly the result of the *Zeitgeist*, or spirit of the times, that has been relevant to the formation of the new religions and their charismatic leaders. No doubt, some of the spirit of political and religious protest of the 1960s has carried over. Increasing attention is focused upon the elimination of social inequality but, more importantly for the new religions, the apparent impediments to self-realization are being attacked by its followers. Second, we have witnessed the development of a widespread need for more intimate social relationships. More than ever before people today are seeking to reduce their feelings of loneliness and despair through participation in small group settings. Third, there is an increasing adolation for charismatic religious leaders, such as Reverend Moon, who seem to epitomize the values and expectations of young religious seekers whose actions are directed toward a religious conversion as a way of undoing their disillusionment and dissatisfaction. These are the young idealists or the "born again" religious converts who become converts of the prophet and his promise of escape from human suffering, inequality, and alienation. To this end, these young people believe that there is an overriding prospect for a better life to be found in cult religion.

Given these conditions, the public will see a continuity of cult leaders and their followers as long as the social conditions that favor the development of cults continues to exist. This is so because when people have feelings that are relatively ambiguous, cult leaders are ready to interpret these feelings as a need for religious salvation. To this extent, it is known that when people are emotionally aroused, they tend to look to other people for a definition of their feelings; charismatic cult leaders seem to take advantage of this situation and label their followers' emotional feelings as appropriate behaviors for faithful converts (Schachter, 1964).

Since the religious seekers' public behavior, like their behavioral commitment to religious practices and proselytization, is self-validating in its effect, when the cultist goes public, in order to support his or her religious ideology, it is highly likely to become increasingly more resistant to outside influence and they are highly likely to "keep the faith." However, a person's public behavior not only binds the individual to the cult group, it also opens up possible attack from the outside community. In a dramatic sense, the cultist's religious beliefs and practices are rendered more irrevocable as his or her freedom to grow psychologically and to accept new and different information is retarded through strong commitment to the cult's theology and ideology.

The dissatisfaction with traditional religion is now, more than ever, diffused throughout youth culture. No longer is it confined to a small minority of religious seekers. The overall picture is one of increasing schism between those young people who eagerly embrace mainstream religious beliefs and those who are seeking a new and different religious experience. The latter are the people who pose a serious threat to more traditional religious precepts and values because many are leaving the church of their parents. In order to understand these issues more fully, I now turn to the topic of commitment to a religious cult lifestyle.

3

Becoming a Cultist: Taking on a Cult Lifestyle and Identity

Traditional religion has not experienced the profound changes during recent years that sect and cult religions have undergone, and those changes that have taken place in religious sects have followed long episodes of extensive revivalism and crusades. This is why we should hesitate to compare traditional religion or sect religion with the dogma and practice of current-day cults. Cults, with their self-styled prophets and exotic beliefs and practices, are not typical religion. Cults, unlike sects, have not crystallized around a religious leader who has emerged from the schismatic division of an established church or denomination. But, as complex and exotic as cults appear on the surface, it is no longer doubtful that many of their leaders are mainly concerned with seeking converts and accumulating great wealth. Perhaps the sharpest contrast between cult religion and traditional religion is that there is a relative absence of these negative characteristics in established churches. It is easy to understand, therefore, how a charismatic cult leader might become an object of criticism from traditional religious groups. The cult leader, unlike traditional religious leaders, is the only source of the follower's salvation. The cult messiahs or gurus may not pray to the same god that traditional priests or ministers do. They may perhaps even reveal themselves to their followers as the only God. This revelation can be a source of strength to the followers, who eventually come to accept him or her as their divine savior.

Faced with what appears to be an unrelenting faith, it can be understood that when people believe in supernatural forces and a cult leader's dream of utopia these beliefs can have a lasting impact on faithful converts. When devotees engage in the cult's deviant behavior and its religious practices many of them have been willing to undergo great hardship and deprivation to maintain their cult membership. Cult leaders and their followers can even sacrifice their lives for their cult, as witnessed by the litany of religious martyrs in recorded history (Braden, 1970). The United States has always had a special feeling for religious leaders and followers, especially those who came from abroad where they suffered from religious persecution. This is why some of the earlier settlers came to America to establish religious based communities of one kind or another. At times, ideologically oriented religions have emerged to play an important role in social change; however, cults and sects have often been treated as an object of moral scorn. This is true because these religious groups have attempted to reprogram society; to make society in the image of the cult. This is also why cult religion holds at best a marginal and apologetic place at the fringes of the greater society (Kephart, 1976; Needleman and Baker, 1978).

How Cults Convert People to Their Beliefs

In recent years, the most visible religious convert to appear in the United States is the born-again convert. Aspirants of religious groups that stress a born-again conversion, no less than their predecessors, seem to regard themselves as the representatives of the only true religion. Hence, in the process of conversion those totally committed undergo drastic change in their religious belief systems. They come to believe that all evil in the world and all of our moral and ethical problems are due to the violation of God's will by humans. The convert is called upon by conscience to represent the precepts and special insights of a spiritual lineage; nevertheless, religious converts often tell about deterioration in traditional moral absolutism and they claim that this is caused by violations found within and without traditional religion.

There is a common and pervasive theme in these new religious groups: a stress on love and acceptance and the promise of personal transformation. In some cults there is an emphasis on mysticism and altered states of consciousness. For example, Hare Krishnas and the Divine Light Mission both practice the teachings of Hindu scriptures (*the Bhagavad-Gita*) and they employ meditative techniques to reach a state where their followers claim that negative mental states are suppressed. When East meets West there is a religious model offered over and above the traditional Western religious theme of the born-again convert.

In a strict sense, cults have their own unique belief systems, their own practices, and their own rituals. However, when a new religious cult has entered the arena, adherents of more traditional religion have attempted to discredit it; this indeed has been the general reaction of established religion to the emergence of the cult movement.

In spite of the mounting criticism of religious cults, established religions seems to be losing their hold as more and more of their church members wander off to seek more meaningful secular or spiritual experiences. This parallel growth in secularism and cultism, and the exodus from traditional religion, has left many clergy and lay ministers frustrated and worried. Some clergy have wondered how otherwise intelligent and rational people can follow self-proclaimed gods. Many clergy members have a difficult time understanding why these young cult devotees are required to turn control of their lives over to the cult group or to the guru for ready-made friendships and love (Stoner and Parke, 1978).

Cult members claim they are ultimately seeking some enlightened discipline to transform their lives into a more meaningful one. Hence, the cult and its leaders treat society as an object of moral scorn — the source of all that's pervasively evil. Whatever the cult persuasion, religious cult aspirants take their new religious experiences seriously. In the final stage of cult conversion the converts' thought processes have been changed, their behavior has been modified, and their beliefs have been changed to fit those of the cult group. This is one of the reasons why some traditional clergy are worried; they feel that "brainwashing, embroidered with trappings of utopian ideals have been used to rebuild the cult's followers" (Cohen 1975).

The sharpest contrast between a cult and a more traditional religious movement is in the way a cult goes about seeking and converting people. When we examine this aspect of the cult movement, it is like opening Pandora's box, for the ultimate discovery encompasses a strange and seemingly bizarre social reality. In the cult's revelation there is an attempt to demonstrate that God's sovereignty has begun again, and it is said to be divinely revealed by the cult leader. It is as if the whole world should know and come to accept the cult's religion and ideology, but first people must allege the chaotic state of current conditions and then recognize the need for a new God: the guru or the messiah (Braden, 1970; Mathison, 1960).

The Logic and the Psychologic of Cult Conversion

One of the first things to happen to the potential cultist is that these disenchanted people begin to feel an increase in their self-respect and they find out that people care enough about them to accept them and love them (Rose, 1970; Zablocki, 1971).

Most cult conversions take place in religious accoutrements, such as revival meetings; for example, those carried out by cult evangelists like Jim Jones or Reverend Moon. The revival meeting is unique in that there is a high degree of persuasive appeal accompanied by intense emotional arousal and elaborate religious ritual. Great stress is placed on the confession of one's sins and wickedness, and the evils of everlasting damnation are brought to bare. Finally, those present are given the "once in a lifetime chance" to expunge their sins and come forth to be saved. The charismatic evangelist does not wait long for members of his or her audience to respond but calls forth particular individuals in order to establish a firm behavioral commitment: the potential convert is required to act on his or her newly found religious beliefs. Following this public display of behavioral commitment, based on the belief that supernatural forces can intervene to improve one's life, great change usually takes place in the convert's lifestyle. As a matter of establishing credibility, faith healing is sometimes staged, and most of the sick and lame appear to become suddenly cured: there is now new hope and self-confidence for all. This is especially true for total converts or those that come to accept the charismatic cult leader as their personal savior. Even though most religious conversion takes place at revival meetings, religious cults have other special ways of attracting and converting members. They concentrate on recruiting and converting children from middle-class homes: those for whom the American dream seems to have been deflated and those who are having problems believing in themselves. Hence, the cult recruiter selects young people who are struggling to find their identity in what appears to be an age of uncertainty (Roof, 1978).

Cult recruiters flatter potential recruits, giving a special kind of false confidence for the disillusioned. They offer the potential convert a weekend devoted to introspection and the opportunity to feel better about one's self. Young people have the chance to look deeper within themselves for some kind of meaning to life. It appears that cult recruiters seem to know who is and who is not a potential cult premie: They are the disillusioned idealists who find the cult appealing because it offers an absolute way to change the world and at the same time escape from their loneliness and alienation (Stoner and Parke, 1978).

From a psychological perspective, most people are unlikely to experience the degree of belief and behavioral change demanded for an intense religious conversion to take place. The exception, perhaps, is found in situations that Robert J. Lifton (1961) labels "brainwashing" or in conditions of *total environment*; for example, the kind of situation that took place in North Korea during the late 1940s and early 1950s. Lifton tells us about the "brainwashing" techniques that were used by Chinese Communists to indoctrinate American prisoners captured during the Korean War, as well as Chinese political prisoners taken during the Chinese Revolution.

Overall, the "brainwashing techniques" used on POWs proved to be only moderately effective in bringing about lasting change in American POW's attitudes and behaviors, nothing like the change reported by observers of the Moonies or Hare Krishna premies. Some experts of the Korean War prefer the term *coercive persuasion* rather than *brainwashing* because the stress was on controlling POW's rewards and punishments and not on classical or Pavlovian conditioning techniques. POWs were separated from their peers and deprived of support for their basic democratic beliefs and values. During this time POWs were encouraged to inform on fellow prisoners. Through deprivation, intensive interrogation, and "thought training," prisoners were expected to develop positive attitudes and beliefs toward their Communist captors. Through public confession of "wrong thinking and doing," and the acknowledgment of more "acceptable beliefs," the group setting was designed to bring about behavioral commitment to a new and different set of political beliefs and values (Schein et al., 1961).

Few situations involve such extreme control of people's lives as those used by the Chinese Communists or the indoctrination techniques used by the Moonies or the Hare Krishna. This is why an understanding of "brainwashing" techniques or "coercive persuasion" should be applicable to a better understanding of the distinctive features of how extensive attitude and belief change takes place in the cult setting. This is especially true of change that takes place through sudden conversion to a cult group's religious beliefs. That is, religious cults demand that recruits experience total change and this highlights the dilemma of the cultists who must convince others of their faith and devotion. These individuals must prove that they have taken on the particular beliefs and values of their cult group. These conditions seem necessary to enhance one's attractiveness or respectworthiness to other cult members; yet, the costs are high because the cult may come to be the only group that is receptive of the convert. Therefore, a cult member cannot easily leave the cult because the cultist is likely to conclude that all worldly problems can be solved by the cult messiah through his promise for a better life.

Against this background one can understand why the convert is lost to the cult group through a peculiar kind of tie to the cult group's exotic beliefs and practices. There is a seeming reduction in acutely felt loyalty and commitment to the outside world. Translated from its religious terms to psychological language, we find considerable influence brought to bear on the convert, and both normative and coercive control are involved. As a result, the cultist's dependency on the group increases. This is why the clinical psychologist, Margaret Thaler Singer (1979) tells us that "leaving a cult means foregoing a sense of brotherhood and a deep sense of intimacy of sharing a very significant experience" (p. 76).

A careful analysis of most cults suggests that their effectiveness in converting people to their dogma depends in part on a balance between making its appeal seem attractive enough and its mission justified enough to potential converts, while at the same time avoiding loss of support from its totally converted members. This is why total converts are required to express public commitment to the cult's beliefs and values, and especially loyalty to and faith in the cult's ideals. This tends to raise all members' level of commitment to their cult. These activities tend to gain sympathy for the cult's appeal from those potential converts present at the time of the call for a cult conversion. Once a potential convert is aroused to an awareness of the cult group's purpose and mission, effective cult conversion still requires an organized effort within the cult group to bring about a strong need to become converted to the cult's dogma. When the cult holds shared beliefs, the cult looks increasingly more attractive to the potential convert. The cult's shared goals can be used to raise the consciousness of those not yet fully committed, as well as those already highly committed to the cult's dogma (Toch, 1965). When this takes place, all aspects of cult life become related to the cult's utopian dream, hence all areas of life become the target of public scrutiny. The demands for unanimity, though they may originate in a purely religious sphere, spill over into the most minute details of daily living of cultists. The cult, led by its messiah, must actively work to achieve their utopia, not merely wait for its survival. They must be willing to do anything to achieve their utopian goals. William Kephart (1976) contends that cult and sect people have always been intrigued by the possibilities of a better life. He notes that some of them have attempted to establish the kind of world they desire by inventing the most extreme form of utopias. Others have even given up on the idea of the perfect life here on earth and have sought this goal in another world or in heaven. In other words, when members of cults feel oppressed, they typically band together as a community, searching for the good and perfect life. Most cult members try to show that a better world exists by the example of their own lifestyle even though most utopian-type communities have not always had the success that its members expected or its leader prophesied (Kephart, 1976).

Although there seems to be some disagreement among critics, most observers agree that cult members are plagued by transcient dissatisfaction. They place their fate in the seemingly benevolent hands of a cult leader and often fail to take precautions against overcommitment and loyalty that members of traditional churches do. At best, some cult members continue to explore alternative lifestyles until they choose what promises social justice and personal happiness. But cult people are determined people, which accounts for the great numbers of cult devotees who become victims of "fanatic" cult indoctrination techniques. Some of these new converts seem simply too willing to conform to the cult's expectations or standards. They vehemently claim that they have willingly become members of their chosen cult, but one suspects that most cultists do not even know what initially influenced them (Singer, 1979).

Against this background, one can easily understand how and why people are attracted to cults. Although it may be difficult to always identify overriding reasons for the cult group's emergence and its great influence in the first place, a few important facts will illustrate the necessary social conditions for the emergence of a cult group. For example, one must first consider the social forces that made it possible for a cult group to oppose traditional religion and set up a counterreligious movement. Having done this, there are certain conditions that must be present to maintain the cult's existence. For example, some religious cults, just as sects, start as splinter groups from more complex and larger religious organizations. This makes them susceptible to great criticism. No doubt, this is why there seems to be a compelling reason for the cult group's adherents to typically attempt to win over others to their faith. To state the situation another way, the cult's religious values and beliefs become polarized and can be the cause of their extreme religious practices and behaviors. There is a failure to incorporate many aspects of traditional religion into their cult beliefs and practices.

A cult group can have a lasting effect on its members, especially those who hold socially and religiously splintered beliefs. Why is this so? First, cults are likely to attract followers under special conditions where people experience uncertainty, anxiety, and frustration. These are the people, who by virtue of their religious beliefs and/or personality dispositions, find that a cult is compatible and consonant with their existing religious and political ideology. The cult group provides the religious mooring the individual is seeking at the precise time that the person is ready to break with past ties. At this time, the person is ready for a new religious involvement and commitment. John Lofland (1966) states that cult religion appeals to people who seem to be predisposed to solve their individual and social problems within a religious framework, whereas most other people are able to work out their personal problems in nonreligious or nonpolitical ways.

The questions remain: How do people become converted to the beliefs of a cult group when their current beliefs seem fundamentally at odds with the beliefs they previously held? And, in such cases, what persuasive techniques do cult leaders use to recruit followers who are not at the time potential candidates but later became faithful representatives of the cult's cause (Zimbardo et al., 1977)? Unfortunately, no comprehensive theory of research data is currently available to fully answer these questions. However, I now turn to information that will reflect in particular on these matters. First, I must examine the nature and relevance of a particular psychological theory to the problem: commitment theory.

Commitment to a Cult Lifestyle

Why do some people choose to join a cult while others do not? One reason that I have just suggested is that there is a failure to perceive other alternatives to solve personal or social problems. Also, additional conditions may be involved. For example, not all those who join cults do so because they are disillusioned and disenchanted with more conventional religious groups or because they are unable to accept the values and beliefs of traditional religion. Some forms of cult conversion are accomplished by converts who seek out a young person sitting alone and accost him with questions like "Do you read the Bible?" "Is God part of your life?" "How do you feel about all of the sin and corruption in the world?" The potential convert is then given an invitation to the religious group's communal house, and then the pressure to join becomes more intense. They question the person's sense of well-being and identity and compare his present lifestyle to the glory of pursuing God's work. All of the group's efforts are focused on the potential convert and on persuading him or her to join the group and experience God first hand (Rice, 1976).

Although people may never find a religious group that is compatible to their social needs, they may continue their search. And, undoubtedly, at this point many processes are likely to be involved; for example, to the extent that a person's beliefs, values, and social needs are undermined, he or she may become even more likely to turn to unconventional groups for solutions to problems or as a way to seek alternative ways to view himself as well as society. What about individuals whose basic assumptions about the world are dichotomized? In this case, their views may reflect an almost complete lack of tolerance for ambiguity: their beliefs may suggest that everything is either absolutely true or false; people are either good or bad; the world is sinful or not; a spiritual value lies in the immediate future — inevitable or impossible; there is one right religion and all else is false; etc. These may be "warning signs," and they are increasingly spotted nowadays in many people who eventually become cult members (Lofland and Stark, 1965; Zimbardo et al., 1977).

The struggle to make one's life or the world into what is construed as a better place demands *effort* and especially *commitment* to clearly defined goals. Charles A. Kiesler (1971) states that when one first becomes committed to an inconsistent or dissonant act (i.e., joining a cult group), one does not have to completely agree with the group's values and beliefs. The person must do something that changes or neutralizes the chosen action or he or she must change the attitudes that produced the inconsistency in the first place. In this case, the individual is likely to justify the action or decision to join the group. However, if the person is already highly committed to the action or decision — and this is more or less consistent with attitudes or beliefs prior to joining the group — further commitment (in effect) is likely to make the action less subject to change. To state it another way, a potential cult recruit's actions will be more resistant to change if he or she has never been required to make a decision to act against them in the first place. This is why the impact of commitment depends on perceiving that one has free-ly taken some kind of action on one's convictions or beliefs, such as joining a cult group—not on being forced to do so.

Kiesler defines *commitment* as a pledging or binding of the in-dividual to behavioral acts. He notes that commitment can be in-creased by increasing one or more of the following factors: (a) By making the act unambigious and public; (b) by increasing the im-portance of an act for the individual; (c) by rendering the act ir-revocable and making it more difficult to undo; (d) by encouraging the person to perform the act because this will increase the person's commitment to the action; and (e) the more freedom (or choice) the person perceives in performing an act, the more likely he or she will become committed to the action of his or her choice.

In line with Kiesler's theory, we know that people's beliefs and behavior are affected frequently by the course of everyday events. For example, a person might decide to leave home or work and, at some point in this transition, it may become all but impossible for the individual to experience a change of mind. In this case the per-son has behaved in a way that has great personal importance and it would be difficult to deny the meaningfulness of any action or to change what is already done. These instances in which a person's own behavior is relatively resistant to change is what I mean by *behavioral commitment*.

Hence, once young people have made a commitment to join a religious cult, they cut themselves off from alternative courses of action. When this happens, new or different considerations are not open and, in this sense, they can become irrational because they de-fend the chosen course of action. If the price for the consequence of making a decision later on becomes aversive, people are likely to build "defenses" against outside influence that suggests the action was wrong. In other words, people can run into trouble once they have made a strong commitment to behave in an irrational manner. For instance, consider a young person, who has agreed to come for a weekend retreat, spending some time with seemingly accepting and loving friends, he or she may find that as time goes by that he or she is unable to impress the group unless he or she becomes more enthused about them. If the group seems attractive enough, com-mon sense would suggest that little influence is needed to win him or her over. And as long as the potential cult convert feels free to continue on in the group, he or she is more likely to develop a strong commitment to the group's goals. Hence, the cult's relative nonacceptance of an individual only makes him or her try all the more for their acceptance. Ironically, then, the worse the cult's members treat a person, the more it will tend to win the person over in the long run. This is what I mean when I say that joining a cult and becoming committed to its goals is not always a rational process, and often former cult members do not remember how they became attracted to a cult (Singer, 1979).

Having examined the nature of commitment theory in some detail, it should be realized that the outcome of commitment depends on whether or not people are required to take action or not against their basic beliefs and values. In short, Kiesler's theory would suggest that when cultists become highly committed to their cult's beliefs there is a "freezing effect" and the person's cult beliefs and behavioral commitment are more resistent to change. In other words, strong commitment to a cult's beliefs tends to bind one to the group's practices and consequently makes one less open to out-side   sources of social influence. This is why seemingly more positive alternative courses of action are all but eliminated for most cultists.

I still need to consider the possible differences between those who end up fully committed to a religious cult and those who manage to leave before total commitment takes place. When I focus my atten-tion on those who become totally committed, and compare them with those less likely to develop a strong commitment to a cult, several possible differences are suggested. The following seem most obvious: (a) People who become totally committed to a cult have initially more intense religious beliefs than those who do not; (b) totally committed converts have initial beliefs and values that are more compatible with the cult than individuals who may eventual-ly leave the cult owing to lack of commitment to its goals; (c) members who are totally committed are more likely to have found greater social support and acceptance in the cult setting than those who are less committed; and, (d) those who remain in the cult, and finally become total converts, have beliefs and values that are more salient to them and they act upon these beliefs, whereas those who leave the cult are relatively unaware of any conflict in their beliefs and values (Fishbein and Ajzen, 1975).

In order to examine these matters in more detail, I will now turn to still another example of how commitment theory can help us understand how a person can become converted to even the most "bizarre" kind of religious cult.

More on Commitment Theory and Cultism

In order to examine in more detail how commitment operates, I will now consider a hypothetical case of a recently converted cult member. Let us assume that the person's verbal commitment to the group is initially rather high and thus his membership in the cult requires behavioral evidence to support the verbal commitment. Further, my example deals with a recruit who is induced by cult members and their leader to publicly espouse the cult's belief that an appeal to supernatural forces is the best way to depict reality or to solve personal or social problems. Let us assume that this action is not great enough to convince the person to make a total religious conversion because his faith needs to be more fully tested: for example, the convert may need to be asked to go out and induce others to join the cult and this behavior may be inconsistent with the convert's beliefs concerning proselytizing others for the cult's cause. However, if the convert proselytizes for the cult without great pressure to do so he will need little, if any, external justification for his behavior because in this case the convert may be highly likely to feel personally responsible for increasing the cult's membership. That is, if the convert can succeed in convincing himself that his actions are not so very far from what he believes is correct, then he will have reduced dissonance. His proselytizing behavior will no longer be inconsistent. Nonetheless, in my example I do not want to imply that the premie, under these conditions, will suddenly become an avowed cultist. What I do mean is that the premie might begin to feel more positive toward his cult membership. In other words, if the potential convert does in fact convince others to join the cult, he is more likely to increase his dedication to the cult's cause. This is why recruits, who work compulsively for their cult, become increasingly more committed to its ideology and more resistant to influence from the outside world. In this way, the "true believer" has found a cause at last, a way to undo all that is wrong with the world. Yet the maintenance of one's cult membership alone may not be enough for total conversion to a cult to take place. However, in this case, devotion to the cult, and revolt against society's values, are thus the conditions which provide the impetus for one's cult conversion.

Similarly, it is not unusual to hear a religious cult's activists express their willingness to give all to their cult, to suffer from severe forms of deprivation, and still indicate that everything they do stems from their strong need for their struggle for freedom and for a cult redemption. At times it appears that some cult members engage in "masochistic-like" behavior, whereby they expect to bring about their own pain and degradation; they "turn the cheek" with the expectation of receiving a slap. Their cult teaches that it is necessary to submit to privation and this requires a renunciation of worldly pleasures as preconditions for attainment of the perfect life of eternal bliss. The cult offers some people, weighted down by a sense of powerlessness and despair, a new hope for salvation where happiness is presumed to be a cult experience. These changes in the premie's outlook have caused religious seekers, and especially young people, to be caught up between two contradictory ways of life, the old one of alienation and unhappiness, the new one of a more promising lifestyle.

Because a particular cult movement sometimes shows little resemblance to any other form of religious movement, I should be more explicit about what I mean when I say that cults convert people through a process of commitment to the cults' ideology and practice. To this point, Rosabeth Moss Kanter (1972) tells us that *involvement* in or *commitment* to a religious group can best be explained through an application of *commitment mechanisms*. These mechanisms operate to attract people to religious groups and they contribute to the longevity of the group. For example:

1. *Sacrifice* is involved when a person is asked to forego the pleasures of mundane life (sex, drinking, and smoking), in order to join a religious

group. This process is related to what Aronson and Mills (1959) call "severe initiation," suggesting that those who suffer the most to obtain membership and acceptance in a group come to value the group more than those who suffer the least.

2. *Investment* takes place when one is asked to sign over his or her property to the group, or to give his or her life savings for the cause, without likelihood of subsequent reimbursement.

3. *Renunciation* takes place when one is isolated from his or her greater community. For example, the cult may demand that its members reject or ignore the mass media, forego family ties, and totally accept the lifestyle of the cult. This is generally done to develop a sense of heightened group cohesiveness, a feeling of "we," or to develop ingroup feelings. This type of commitment mechanism is likely to produce feelings of outgroup hostility (Dion, 1973; Sherif and Sherif, 1953).

4. *Communion* among members takes place because a religious group is likely to recruit people from common backgrounds, who have similar beliefs and values. Along this line, there is evidence that people are more attracted to those who are similar to themselves in values, beliefs, and attitudes (Berscheid and Walster, 1978).

5. *Mortification* takes place when members are required to publicly confess their past sins. Group criticism of the sinner is employed to punish publicly the group's deviant members (Zimbardo et al., 1977).

6. *Transcendence* takes place in the group when religious ritual is used to bring about cult-group cohesiveness. In this case cult groups have great investment in spiritual activities, like meditation. Transcendence tends to make members of a religious group feel that they are an integral part of their community (Lofland and Stark, 1965).

Because of the dominant role of commitment, Kanter's "commitment mechanisms" can be used to account for the heightening of cult-group cohesion that takes place as members become totally converted to the cult's accepted lifestyle.

Apart from Kanter's "commitment mechanisms," studies dealing with the effects of intense cult living show that when people are converted to a cult they experience great changes in their attitudes and beliefs. But what specific changes do in fact take place in a convert's sense of meaning or lifestyle? Following conversion, does an individual shift his or her actual value preferences so that his or her religious values become more important and more salient, acting as guides for his or her behavior? Research on these matters is sketchy; however, a recent study, reported by Crandall and Rasmussen (1975), of those who had just experienced a religious conversion showed that these people changed their values and they changed to a more positive purpose in life.

Since Milton Rokeach's (1973) value inventory shows a strong relationship between a person's values and specific behaviors, Crandall and Rasmussen (1975) reasoned that values are central to a person's purpose in life. These researchers, as expected, found that the value salvation was positively related to a positive purpose in life, whereas the materialistic values of pleasure, excitement, and comfort were found to be negatively correlated to purpose in life. Then, as was expected, those who had undergone a religious conversion valued their religious salvation more than they valued materialistic interests. In a similar study, Soderstrom (1976) found that the converts he studied not only increased their purpose in life, following a nontraditional religious conversion, but they also were more willing to proselytize for their religious cause.

At first glance, the above research seems relatively straightforward; however, a word of caution is needed: these studies do not directly show that a premie's religious values determine his or her behavior. To demonstrate that they do, the researcher would have to show that changes in values produce changes in behavior. But, what do we actually learn, on a psychological level, when it is observed that changes in a premie's behavior have taken place following a religious cult conversion? On a short-term basis, members of the new religions generally speak of a feeling of being "filled by the spirit of God." Using this level of personal testimony, writers report that converts talk about a meaningful transformation in their lives and there is an adoption of a "new lifestyle" based upon religious teachings (Stoner and Parke, 1978).

Cults as Reference Groups

Unfortunately, little evidence is available to describe in much detail precisely what initial changes take place in cultists' attitudes or feelings; however, Mary White Harder, James T. Richardson, and Robert B. Simmonds (1976) report on Christ Commune (a pseudonym for a branch of the Jesus movement), where most of the members are white high school graduates in their early twenties. They previously held low paying, boring jobs and came from affluent homes where their parents' religion did not have much impact on their lives. The social organization of this Jesus Commune is such that females seem to "know their place." Submission to males and the Lord's teachings is stressed. Males and females are encouraged to control their "sexual impulses," and courtship and marriage are regulated by a group council. Life in the group is simple, based on long hours of hard work and frequent group readings on the Bible.

Harder et al. measured the commune's members' attitudes toward alcohol, drugs, tobacco, and premarital sex before joining the commune and again several months after joining. They found that members had significantly shifted from a liberal position to a relatively conservative stance on all of the above attitudinal issues. In addition, the researchers observed that the commune was "successful in winning and keeping its converts." This "success" was attributed to a strong emphasis on communal living, hard work, and social isolation in a setting where the group's norms for noncompetition, antiintellectualism, and total acceptance of the group's religious dogma were made salient.

The kind of change that emerges from members of the Jesus Commune model is one that has a special meaning for its members. This model is especially interesting because similar changes have been reported by those who join religious cults like the Moonies or the Hare Krishna (Cohen, 1975). The demands on the premie begin with a cult membership and become increasingly more complex as the person experiences a total cult conversion. The cult becomes an important reference group for the premie. Reference groups are those persons whom the premie utilizes as a standard to judge his own behavior.

Reference groups (like cults) operate to influence members in at least three ways: First, they specify expected behavior, direct attention to them, and set the rules for conformity. Second, the comparison reference group shows how to engage in expected behavior. Third, other people respond to the person's behavior and either approve or disapprove of it.

Groups that are most likely to exert great influence on us through strong pressure are our reference groups: the people with whom we most identify and to whom we look to for social approval and as guides or standards for our behavior. Often we are simply a member of a reference group through definition, such as ethnic, racial, or religious identity. However, people may actively seek out a given reference group, such as a cult, because the group seems to control various value resources, for example, social acceptance and friendship.

When a person becomes a member of a cult reference group, he or she usually comes to strongly adhere to the standards for behavior set by the group. Perhaps the most evident characteristic of any religious cult is the set of devices through which it attempts to bring about uniformity of beliefs and behaviors of its members. This is no less true of religious groups that are part of one's community than it is for one's "ordinary" association groups; however, it is more obvious in a cult. For example, during the 1930s Theodore Newcomb (1943) investigated the impact of a college reference group on influencing students' attitudes and behavior and demonstrated the crucial importance of a reference group in shaping their views. Between 1935 and 1939, the entire student body at Bennington College (Vermont) was studied with respect to the change that took place in their attitudes and behavior, as well as their assimilation into the college community. Newcomb was particularly interested in what factors determine changes in political and economic beliefs when students become highly involved and commited to their immediate community.

Most Bennington students were from upper-middle-class families. The school was isolated from any urban area, and students lived on campus in houses of about twenty girls each. They ate in a common dining room and did their course work and extra-curricular activity in common. Especially interesting were the close student-faculty relationships: classes were small, only six or eight students. Student government focused upon the responsibility of both faculty and students to make decisions. Generally school policies were derived from these committees. In all respects, according to the time (and even today), the school was by definition liberal. It was here that Newcomb taught and carried out his several years of research on students' attitudes and beliefs. Political liberalism at that time meant favorable attitudes toward Franklin D. Roosevelt's New Deal, whereas conservatism was viewed as opposition to the New Deal and defense of the status quo.

To begin with, Newcomb found that great attitudinal change took place in Bennington students during their four years of college. That is, the entering students became more liberal in political and economic attitudes with each year of college, providing that they did not drop out and return home. This pattern of liberalization tended to persist several years after the students left Bennington. Follow-up research, twenty-five years after these young women had graduated, showed that the Bennington graduate's attitudes and beliefs remained relatively stable over a twenty-five year period (Newcomb et al., 1967).

Even though the situation at Bennington during the 1930s was much different from what I have said about contemporary religious cults, Newcomb's research does indeed illustrate how attitude change takes place in a community where individuals interact closely over relatively long periods of time.

What was there about Bennington that set the stage for change that can also be found in a more intense degree in a modern cult setting? The following seem obvious: (a) students were isolated from any direct influence from their outside community; (b) they lived in a setting that encouraged a high degree of intimate interaction; (c) the impact of the college community was not equally influential for all students, some of the students did not accept the school's liberal values and beliefs (a careful analysis of cults shows that not all recruits undergo total conversion to the cult's religious beliefs or political ideology); and (d) those that took part in student and faculty activities were highly sensitive to participation in the college community, and, no doubt, became more highly committed to the values of the college (this is also true of cultists who participate in the cult's ritual and practices).

Since groups (such as cults and, to a lesser degree, college settings such as Bennington) regulate both diversity and uniformity within a group setting by prescribing the rules of conduct, these group standards provide valuable information to the individual about matters that cannot easily be dealt with independently. The group member may act like others in the situation because he or she is uncertain how to do otherwise. The group's standards for conduct are highly likely to be a key to the acceptance of group members. However, when one adheres to the group's expectations, there is an obvious advantage to be gained; one can satisfy one's own personal needs and goals because the reference group provides approval and acceptance. On a more specific level, the cult's norms not only act to regulate members' behavior within the cult's setting but also to innoculate members from possible influence from the noncult world. It is here that the willingness of people to deny, ignore, or normalize their views depends on how their cult membership affects them personally.

Although Newcomb's study is informative, I hasten to caution against generalizing the results too far. When we compare the kinds of things that elicit change in a college setting with those of a cult group several significant differences emerge: people found in a college setting do not always face the kind of pressure to change that takes place in a cult setting. That is, sometimes people do not change to a great degree because they are in a situation that does not demand great and lasting change. However, in the process of examining the cult group's influence on its members' attitudes, beliefs, and behaviors, great change can take place even in a relatively short time. In the case of cults, a reorganization of the person's religious beliefs takes place, whereas Bennington students changed their political and economic beliefs more than they did their religious beliefs. Nevertheless, the process of change is similar.

When cultists or college students, like Bennington's women, experience great involvement in their group, the stage is set for significant attitude and behavioral change. This apparently takes place in a special setting where people are first isolated from their family and past associates and especially where deep and lasting relationships develop. In such situations strong social pressure produces lasting change in the direction of the group's values and beliefs. However, whether or not a person becomes strongly committed to his or her beliefs or behavior depends on what kind of values and goals are set by the leader for the group. Needless to say, unlike most groups, many cults exhibit "extremism" and "fanaticism." We must remember, however, that cultists were exposed to these kinds of beliefs in the first place.

Dederich for the Misbegotten:
The Synanon Model for Radical Change

In an effort to provide some insight into the seemingly exotic behavior of cultists, I might best begin by examining the strong social influence that produce these results in another example of what people are actually saying and doing. This time I will discuss Synanon's model for change, used to get the drug and alcohol addict back on the "straight and narrow path." Here I will attempt to show how Synanon's model is related to the cult model for drastic personality and behavioral change.

Before I describe the Synanon movement, I should hasten to point out that most people seem to want to live more self-fulfilling lives; however, to accomplish this not all people are willing to risk personal freedom, gamble on a new lifestyle, or take a chance with what might be construed as an extreme group. The story changes when drug or alcohol addiction is a source of shame and is associated with deep feelings of anxiety and fear. In this case, it seems wise to discontinue use of drugs or alcohol if all that is required is to give one's loyalty to a charismatic therapist. When this happens, however, one can lose the sense of personal freedom, and the analogy to the cultist becomes obvious. This is true because when one turns to the charismatic therapist (or cult leader), the potential for manipulation is especially great when one completely trusts the therapist (or cult leader) and pledges complete loyalty and obedience to the group. Caught up in the web of group commitment, the person starts "tuning in" to what others are saying and doing. This can be especially dangerous when others become fanatic in their beliefs and "extreme" in their behaviors.

In 1958, Charles E. Dederich, although confronting great skepticism from mental health professionals, established a group he labeled *Synanon*. Despite these drawbacks, a group of people who ostensibly were concerned with curing their drug habit and improving their life, were invited to live at Synanon.

According to popular reports, Dederich's Synanon employs a special form of group therapy where three male and three female patients plus a Synanist leader (usually a moderator) attempt to get at what they contend are conscious and unconscious stratagems people use to avoid the cold, hard truth about themselves. The group uses ridicule, a kind of cross-examination, and even aggressive attacks on patients in order to accomplish therapy. The drug addict is encouraged to experience an emotional catharsis. In order to encourage a cathartic release, the Synanon group creates the kind of situation many patients fear most: loss of self-control. While all this is going on, the Synanist leader does not in any way attempt to convince the drug addict that he or she is a stable individual.

The Synanists use many other devices to change or control the addict's beliefs and behavior; for example, they employ "haircut sessions." That is, members of the Synanon family take apart, either constructively or destructively, the addict's performance in front of the group's family. Followers of Dederich claim that the "haircut" produces a dramatic change in addicts' attitudes and especially their subsequent group performance. when this does not seem to work, a figurative haircut is followed by a literal haircut. The addicts' head are completely shaved.

What characterizes the day-to-day life of the Synanon family? Lewis Yablonski (1967) contends that the family, much like the religious cult, is more or less autocratic and that members engage in a wide range of family activities such as house cleaning and cooking. But what is the Synanon model for change? For many it is as great as the change that takes place in religious cults. For example, a negative self-image and low self-esteem, prominent in both Synanon members and cult converts, are attacked when the individual is given a chance to resolve this dilemma through developing a more positive self-image.

But, not many people are willing to take this kind of risk to establish close relationships. Some people who feel anxious prefer to be alone and not with others (Sarnoff and Zimbardo, 1961). Nevertheless, once the individual decides to solve his problems in the Synanon family, intense relationships develop and even stronger attachments eventually take place. When this happens, the

Synanon family can become even more demanding and more cruel, but the addict's devotion to the group remains steadfast (Yablonski, 1967).

The kind of behavior elicited from Synanon addicts must be highly motivated by the desire for change. The major source of this change seems to stem from the discontent felt by the drug addicts, especially with specific situations they seem to get themselves into and dissatisfaction with their drug habit and troublesome lifestyle. However, the focus at Synanon is not so much upon the main problem (drug or alcohol addiction), but on the lasting impact that the Synanon family is to have on the individual. Because many of the Synanon members have brought with them a myth of not being able to change, they find something positive in their misery and hardship in the group. In this case we know that Synanon draws its members from those people who seem to have encountered problems without answers much like people who seek solutions in religious cult settings and they seem all too willing to pay the price for a new identity or the promise for a new and better life.

What lesson can be learned from Dederich's drug addicts? First, they must not only recognize that Synanon requires total commitment to the rigid rules set for treatment, but they must also realize that, in the guise of "group paternalism," the family sets the conditions for role-determined behavior. The addict must conform to the group's expectations or suffer the consequences (punishment). Second, although there are episodes of hesitation to accept the Synanon family's strategy for "treatment," Dederich's addicts seem to invariably regain their faith each time they enter the family circle.

Cult members seem to experience some of the same kinds of *turning points* as Synanon addicts in their increased self-awareness and desire to take some action with their personal problems. This takes place for both the Synanon addict and for the cult member under circumstances where old obligations and ties diminish and are replaced by a new involvement in a totally isolated group setting.

By reading accounts of Synanon addicts, one can begin to understand the fury that many people who join the family must arouse in themselves for having committed themselves to such extreme forms of treatment or therapy. However, if one delves a bit deeper into the Synanon movement, one can easily see that this approach to changing people's beliefs and behavior is considerably more complex than some of us would guess. For example, a constant theme of the Synanon family is that the drug addict gains "power through passivity and dependence." The application of psychological principles to change addicts, like coercive persuasion, has ramifications that are likely to extend far beyond the relatively short time spent in therapy. For example, the addicts come to find out that their beliefs about personal control are differentially related to motivational factors rather than the addicts' ideological makeup. That is, drug addicts who seem to gain a sense of personal control over their lives (internal control) do so at the expense of heightened social and personal demands that seriously question their ability to control the forces that shape their lives (external control).

Synanon attempts radical change in the basic values and self-identities of its addicts. Synanon also attempts to build upon prior values and an apparent need for social and personal control over those forces that determine the addicts' outcomes. In contrast, then, the aim of the cult is to demand that the convert prepare for functioning in the cult group by taking the role of the "born again" convert, who will live in the religious cult and not bend to outside influence where evil, sin, and corruption are said to prevail. The cult members' status in the group demands that they accept totally the norms or standards of the cult leader, which, of course, stresses values and beliefs at odds with mainstream or more conventional religious groups. To this extent, the cult group creates a form of deviance. However, when we consider Dederich's addicts, additional factors have to be taken into account if one is to understand social change because perhaps, most important of all, the addict is required to learn new ways of dealing with old problems and then eventually return to society and live with what cultists label sin, evil, and corruption.

It is no secret that methods of self-criticism and the apparent "masochism," practiced by Dederich's addicts and the "mind control techniques" practiced by a cult leader are similar. Religious converts, like Dederich's addicts, become totally dependent on their leader and menial labor, loyalty, and absolute obedience to the messiah or the guru are given in exchange for ready-made friendship and social support. Synanon members treat their drug or alcohol addiction and in the process become "converted" to Dederich's lifestyle, just as religious cultists who work for the cause become converted to the cult's expectations.

Once the initial decision is taken to join an "extreme" or "fanatic" group, the rest comes easy because critical thinking and rational self-evaluation are set aside once the group has won the battle for one's mind. Under these conditions it is difficult to see how people can alleviate their problems only at the expense of a utopian dream that will slowly die. Central to this view of the utopian dream one needs only to turn to what has been described as the most bizarre tragedy of our time — People's Temple mass suicide-murder — in order to illustrate the saga of a cult that embraced everything I have been saying about the potential for cult fanaticism and self-destruction.

People's Temple: The Saga of a Cult That Killed Itself

I have discussed cults basically from a psychological point of view. I have said that potential cult members, like most others, seek out similar others because of the rewards and intimate interaction they anticipate from those who hold similar religious beliefs. In this sense, cultists seem to anticipate that their feelings of frustration and despair will somehow be alleviated through their cult experience. This is not the whole story, unfortunately. If people believe that a cult is the answer they are likely to exaggerate its importance and underrate their own capacity to solve problems. Hence, the cult group atmosphere of "love bombing," acceptance, congeniality, and its resulting group cohesiveness, may come at great costs to the individual's psychological well-being. When this happens, the cult member may be in danger of losing sight of a social reality seemingly more reasonable and more rational. This is so because the cult can easily take on a group quality that paradoxically makes the group more important than the individual. I will examine what can take place when the group's goals seem to mask the psychological needs of its members.

One of the basic ideas behind a cult that moves in an extreme or fanatic direction is that, through commitment, people can do irrational and deviant things. But, it must be remembered that when a

cult is threatened from outside its members can become acrimoni-
ous and motivated to safeguard their way of life. Strong commitment to the group can even culminate in death. For example, over
900 members of People's Temple who left California and settled in
the rain forrest of Guyana, South America, committed suicide
under the direction of Reverend Jim Jones, apparently in order to
save the cult from the threat of outside destruction. Just how could
over 900 persons be led to mass suicide? In order to suggest an
answer to this perplexing question, I will trace the chain of events
leading to the Jonestown suicide-massacre. Nobody seemed to
notice the beginning of a tragedy when Reverend Jim Jones was ordained as a minister in the state of Indiana. After a long time of
what Jones felt was undue harrassment and religious persecution,
he left Indiana and eventually established People's Temple in San
Francisco. Once Jones settled in San Francisco, he told his followers
that they were going to experience freedom, equality, and love. For
a time they did, and they became increasingly more favorably
disposed to Jones' religious dogma and practices. After some time,
however, his followers found that he demanded total and complete
loyalty from them and made them give their property and money
to the Temple. While all this was taking place, Jones demanded that
he be the object of total worship; his charismatic style and his ability to influence others, no doubt, contributed to his feelings of self-
importance.

At first glance, the story of Jim Jones seems confusing because
the more his followers seemed to support his cult, the more
suspicious he became of those whom he felt did not give him total
and complete loyalty. He became especially suspicious of those
who opposed his religious teachings and practices. Just as Jones was
to become exposed to the world as a phoney, he left San Francisco
and led his most loyal followers to Guyana, in order to establish his
ultimate utopia: Jonestown or the new People's Temple settlement.

The move from San Francisco to Guyana left Jones and his flock
totally isolated from outside influence. For a time Jonestown
seemed to prosper. During this time, however, Jones became increasingly more irrational and fanatic. Jonestown soon began to
resemble an armed camp; it was almost impossible for members to
come and go freely. It was at this time that Jones initiated a pro-

gram of sleep deprivation and harrassment. His people were underfed and beaten as they were forced to attend long hours of Jones' indoctrination and his "brainwashing sessions." Conditions of extreme fatigue, overwork, and poor physical health contributed to the converts' feelings of powerlessness and indecision. Jim Jones even led his cult group in routine practice suicide sessions. This was done in order to make it clear to his followers that suicide was an acceptable and even desirable solution to a crisis: a way to become a martyr and to blame society for one's own demise.

C. Eric Lincoln and Lawrence H. Mamiya (1980) indicate that Jonestown reflected the idea of a political religion because Jim Jones believed in what they label *apostolic socialism*, or the quest for social justice through the establishment of a socialist utopia. They note that some of Jones' members joined his movement for political reasons and not because of their strong religious convictions. Reverend Jones himself proposed a Marxist ideology, yet he stressed the religious aspects of his cult movement. Lincoln and Maimya even consider the Guyana mass suicide an example of *revolutionary suicide* ("suicide for socialism"); a reaction against the death of Congressman Ryan and the possible legal action against Jones.

Even at this writing, the question still remains why over 900 people followed Jim Jones in mass suicide. That is, we still do not know for sure what were the more immediate causes of the Guyana mass suicide. We know that following the assassination of California's Congressman Leo Ryan, who came to visit and investigate the reported poor living conditions of Jonestown, and the desertion of a few otherwise faithful cult members, Jones was overwhelmed with paranoidlike feelings of despair. As a final desperate act, he assembled his cult at a central pavilion and continued to urge them to die for the cause. Finally, Jim Jones demanded, under conditions of threat, mass suicide and then potential dissidents and detractors were shot. The unforgetable, grotesquerie of mass suicide and massacre ended in death by Kool-Aid laced with cyanide, as Jim Jones became the victim of his own paranoia. For the most part, we are told that many of Jones' cult members apparently went to their death willingly and even joyously; they were unable to resist (Krause, 1978; Lincoln and Mamiya, 1980).

The apparent idealism of Jones' followers, coupled with their feelings of despair and helplessness, no doubt, contributed to their willingness to follow him to South America. Once there they were made totally dependent upon Jones. They had given all of their material possessions to People's Temple, whose dogma and values seemed at the time to match their own, and finally one suspects that death became a special kind of demise: a means to enter another world of everlasting peace.

My odyssey through what has been labeled the suicide cult seems to confirm what I have said about a cult's potential for fanaticism. This underscores the ultimate danger of a cult experience where the guileless find themselves entangled in a web of self-destruction.

Because one of the major conditions present in "extreme" cults, like People's Temple, is total control by the group, I suggest here that coercive persuasion, long hours of sleep deprivation, and feelings of despair played on Jones' converts' innermost fears and anxieties. In such cases there is greater stress placed on correct feelings than on one's reason and intellect. Religious doctrine takes precedence over other forms of reality and it is here that the values of the individual, compared to values of the cult group, are diminished and, as just demonstrated, the insidious result can result in fanaticism and self-destruction.

In conclusion, I have tried to show that membership in a religious cult springs from many sources. I have demonstrated that there is a relationship between the special kind of events that confront the potential convert and the attraction of a particular cult movement. In this connection, people should remember that membership in a cult is often self-validating and this is why the cult competes successfully for the loyalty of its members. They should also take note that, clearly, the process of cult conversion is a complex problem; however, among the more important aspects of a religious cult that people should keep in mind is that even though the goals of a cult are often viewed with skepticism by the outside observer, members of the cult take their cult membership seriously: they believe it to the extent of abandoning their families, sacrificing their jobs, school, and their material possessions; yes even giving their lives to protect their cult lifestyle and their cult leader.

If people are to take religious cults seriously, it would seem necessary that they at least should consider their history. We would do well to remember that cults have emerged from a common form of social unrest, sometimes only fragmentary while at other times quite obvious. Taken in this sense, it is important and revealing to note that widespread religious and spiritual uneasiness seemed to emerge during the early part of this century. This is when many cult and sect leaders clearly divorced themselves from traditional religion. However, the close connection between the current cult movement and traditional religion has only a relatively short history. Nevertheless, when one considers the recent appeal of cults, one also becomes aware of their unsalutory change because the cult scene is now dominated by what is labeled religious "kooks and quacks." This is why, in order to gain some historical perspective to the current "cult movement," I will discuss its roots in my search for a *cult prototype*.

4

Roots of the Cult Belief System and the Current Diversity of Cults

The Cult Movement and the Ebb and Flow of a Historical Perspective

Cults, like most total environments, have shortcomings. Some cults can bring out the worst in people. Philosopher Friedrich Nietzsche even claimed that madness often characterizes what he labeled extreme religious groups. Anthropologist Weston La Barre (1972) contends that: "If anything, group membership often blunts ethical perception and fetters moral imagination" (p. 14). More recently, social psychologist Charles Buys (1978) warned that "extreme groups" can be dangerous to the well-being of members because they can create feelings of *dehumanization* and loss of *self-focus*. Many "radical" groups in history have been viewed as obstacles to rational thinking because they *diffused responsibility* for the group's deviant actions. This is why the cataloging of group-based deviance is depressing to write about and to read about: It underscores a tragedy of the human condition.

Much of the literature of the past few decades has been characteristized by the common assumption that cult groups emerge out of the shared dissatisfactions and anger that are present at any one point in history (Needleman and Baker, 1978). There is also a common theme that cults tend to follow a recurring life cycle. Then, within the context of recent history, is there a parallel in American religion for the emergence of the present status of cults in America? This is an important question since my task in this section is to search for a historical prototype for the present-day cult movement.

I should place the matter of cults in historical perspective because traditionally there is a basic assumption that people's religious beliefs have an inveterate historical origin. This is true even though some present-day cults seem, on the surface, to have developed their own belief systems, practices, and special kind of dogmatic ritual. Nevertheless, it has happened before. This is why it is standard for writers to claim that most present-day cults have their historical prototypes (Cantril, 1963; Kanter, 1972).

The deluge of cults that have flooded the American spiritual arena suggests that in addition to being removed from conventional religion, cults are by no means a new phenomenon in America. They are one of the earliest expressions of religious dissatisfaction and they show a dedication to religious pluralism. Cults flourished during the 18th and 19th centuries. It was not until the recent surge of "bizarre" and exotic religious movements took hold, however, that they caught the attention of the general public. This happened when a number of colorful hierophants such as Father Divine, Marion Keech, Reverend Moon, and Reverend Jim Jones entered the cult scene.

In spite of their sense of challenge to traditional religion, the problems of today's cults are found in the problems of society. Systematically studied, they follow the resumé of history. There was a time not too long ago that cults were the maidservants of traditional religion. Their major function was to tidy up the household of conventional religious dogma: to challenge traditional religion and to make its theology more palpable or more obvious to greater numbers of people. All this was changed, however, by the irascible and flamboyant cult leaders of recent years. This is why most modern cults are considered critical factions, with little inclination to consider the possibility of merging with mainstream religion or eventually getting back into the fold of the greater social system.

Religious cults, like other religious movements in the world at large, leave evidence of their presence. As a result, the psychologist can use these traces to find out various things about them. For example, a great deal can be learned about cults by simply examining the reasons for their growth and their decay. Probably no one can fully appreciate the present cult movement without placing it in the context of the recent history of cults. When this is done, we will find that the roots of cultism are wide and deep. In the effort to trace the origin of cults, we come inevitably to focus on the seemingly indubitable beginnings of the prototype of the modern cult. All this suggests that an analysis of cults is largely a diversity that stems from the ebb and flow of a religious cult sensibility. Even though the spirit of the age affects the kind of reality and the kind of perspective that emerges as a particular cult theme, all cults seem to have their historical prototype.

Much of the literature of the past four decades can be characterized by the common belief that cult movements emerge from shared dissatisfactions and discontent in a given segment of the population. The cult itself often develops as a vehicle to reduce these dissatisfactions and discontents or to change the society that gave birth to these conditions. The genesis of any cult movement is usually found in enclaves of disillusionment and alienation with the existing social order (Kephart, 1976). Out of the emerging belief that a better life is possible, the religious cult frequently evolves as a vehicle to the attainment of a dream of utopia. Such utopian visions are generally extremely unrealistic when one takes into account that the cult has emerged out of strong opposition to the dominant cultural theme. When the larger society, against which the cult has opposed itself, takes notice of the unrealistic and often radical cry for change, the reasons for the cult's existence is threatened, and even though the cult itself may continue to thrive, its capacity to influence social change is virtually abated. However, few episodes of cult behavior leave a society in which they have taken place untouched by their influence.

From Father Divine to Daddy Jones

In order to discuss the impact that cults have had, it is necessary to take stock of their emerging format. Hadley Cantril (1969) tells us that the late Father Divine's Kingdom of Peace movement can in fact serve as a prototype of the modern cult. For example, Father Divine was truly a living charismatic religious leader, he was demonstrably wealthy, he led his flock in a truly totalitarian style, he was intolerant of traditional religious beliefs, and he promised that his converts could work to save the world from evil and sin. Baker's followers were taught to believe that the outside world was abysmally evil and something to avoid. He devised his cult's ritual and suppressed "negative thoughts" as he encouraged his converts to become dependent on him. But how was Father Divine able to persuade so many people to join his utopian cult? And, what sort of people joined his movement? Before I attempt to answer these questions, I will attempt to uncover the turning of events culminating in Baker's Kingdom of Peace movement. After I have examined the intricacies of Father Divine's movement, I will suggest its relation to some recent cults, mainly Reverend Jim Jones' People's Temple.

George Baker (Father Divine) was born 1880 in Savannah, Georgia, where he was ordained as a traditional black minister. When Baker's congregation dwindled, he left Georgia for Baltimore to save lost souls. While in Baltimore, Baker worked as a gardener during the day and as an assistant preacher at night. It was at this time that he became especially active and gained the reputation of a popular black minister.

Prior to Baker's association with Sammuel Morris, a black minister from Baltimore who taught that "God dwells within every man," there was little if any indication that George Baker was to emerge as a charismatic religious leader. Before this happened, a triumvirate was formed among George Baker, Sammuel Morris, and John Hickerson. All three of these black ministers claimed that they had been reborn and were in fact a reincarnation of Christ. They also claimed that this was the basis for their divine authority. Then, in 1913, after the triumvirate broke up and each black minister went his separate way, George Baker traveled to Valdosta, Georgia to preach the gospel to a large number of black people who thought that he was Christ. It was during this time that several local pastors had Baker arrested and finally taken to court. The charge: "Any individual who believes himself to be God must in point of fact be insane." As a matter of record, a jury declared Baker "insane," and they ordered him to leave the state of Georgia.

Subsequent to this encounter with local ministers, Baker left Georgia with a few faithful converts. In 1915 Baker and his disciples traveled to New York City, finally settling in Brooklyn. While in Brooklyn, Baker attracted several new members to his cult. It was at this time that George Baker decided to call himself Father Divine (Burham, 1963; Cantril and Sherif, 1938).

Father Divine's true believers (total converts) gained economic security, such as lodging, food, and employment, in exchange for their loyalty and obedience to his rigid dogma. For instance, Baker prohibited smoking, drinking, swearing, and sexual behavior. He could make these demands because his followers loved him and they believed in his plans for their salvation. Of course, Father Divine assured his followers that they would have everlasting salvation in exchange for their sacrifices. However, he did not tolerate backsliders, and it is said that he even made his "flock" turn over all of their earnings to him as evidence of commitment to his cause (Kephart, 1978).

Father Divine's cult membership increased, and by the 1930s, after he had imbued thousands of his converts with a sense of hope and purpose through what was described as miraculous cures, the police and countless angry and skeptical citizens demanded Father Divine's ouster. Following these charges, he was indicted and within weeks he became a *cause célèbre*. When a judge imposed a one-year prison sentence and a fine, Father Divine was placed in jail, only to find out that the judge suddenly died of an apparent heart attack. Father Divine took advantage of the situation and declared that: "I hated to do it to the judge." Shortly after the judge died, an appellate court reversed Father Divine's original conviction on the grounds that prejudicial comments had been voiced by the judge who had originally sentenced him to jail. The death of the judge, and the subsequent appellate court decision, increased Father Divine's popularity with the black community. As a result, Father Divine's cult grew, as did his holocaustic prophecies and claim of supernatural power. He launched a more vigorous effort to cure people of arthritis, cancer, heart disorders, and numerous physical disabilities (Cantril and Sherif, 1938; Kephart, 1978).

From a historical perspective, what factors seem most important in the development and turn of events in Father Divine's Kingdom of Peace movement? The following seem obvious: (a) Father Divine offered black people hope during a time of economic depression. During this time blacks were even more alienated from society than today, especially poor blacks. Father Divine engendered self-respect in these people. (b) He rewarded his followers with praise, employment, food, and lodging. He did this for those willing to live according to his religious teachings. He could even punish those who disobeyed him and still they loved and worshiped him. (c) He possessed what leadership experts label charisma. Even his height (he was less than five feet tall) seemed to work to his advantage. His exuded enthusiasm, self-confidence, and possessed persuasive skills, suggesting that he was indeed a leader with high credibility. Most of his followers claimed that Jesus Christ and Father Divine both had a special kind of persuasive skill, matched by high intelligence and insight. (d) He practiced what he preached: he did not smoke, drink, gamble, or use profanity. He even renounced sex and refused to dress in the typical religious ceremonial garb: he wore "just plain business suits."

Father Divine undoubtedly had the best of intentions. His goals and his mission must have seemed imminently reasonable to his followers. Father Divine's seemingly egalitarian beliefs and his accompanying religious ideology were of crucial importance in his followers' lives. No doubt, many disillusioned people who followed him came to tolerate the painful social and economic conditions of the day. Divine helped to reduce, and often eliminated human suffering, and his cult followers responded with strong and persistent attempts to conform to the religious practices of his cult. In light of this phenomenon, proselytizing among members increased and Father Divine's movement grew, and whatever the full explanation, commitment to the cult's belief system increased. Other alternative social realities became less preferable.

My discussion of Father Divine's cult is likely to raise the question of why I suggested earlier that this movement can be considered a prototype of the modern cult. In this regard, the social psychologist Hans Toch (1965) suggests that cult leaders often model their leadership style after former cult leaders. This suggests that cult leaders, like Father Divine, can have a strong and lasting influence. For example, Reverend Jim Jones' People's Temple was in part modeled after Father Divine's Kingdom of Peace movement. "Daddy" Jones often quoted Father Divine and he even preached the same kind of sermons. Jones attempted to instill dignity and self-respect in his converts, just as Baker had done; however, Jones' cult was more fanatic than Baker's group (Lincoln and Mamiya, 1980).

Father Divine's Kingdom, with its strange eschatological dogma and its ritualized practices, must have seemed appealing for hundreds of people who received Father's blessing. I can guess that many of today's poor people and today's disillusioned youth would be tempted by Divine's cult appeal. As a matter of fact, Reverend Jim Jones and Father Divine both appealed to many of the same kind of people, even though historical distance separated these cult leaders.

Father Divine's flamboyant cult, no doubt, has been the model (prototype) for many contemporary cults. Divine's cult not only had many of the characteristics of present-day cults, but more importantly his cult has left its traces in the history of new religious movements. For example, it is known that Father Divine's movement was as great a media event as Reverend Moon or Reverend Jim Jones. This is why an awareness of the Kingdom of God movement is particularly illuminating (Lincoln and Mamiya, 1980).

In the 1950s, Jim Jones attended a service conducted by the then aging Father Divine. Later Jones changed his style of preaching. Like Father Divine, Reverend Jones demanded that his followers call him "Father" or "Dad." Jones even encouraged his followers to call his wife Marceline "Mother Jones." Father Divine forced his followers to call his wife "Mother Divine." Both Jones and Baker represented absolute authority and demanded obedience from their converts. Both George Baker and Jim Jones had their greatest influence on people who were victims of despair and a low self-image. The depression years of the 1930s gave impetus to Father Divine's movement, whereas the chaos of the 1960s and 1970s, brought about by the civil rights movement and the Vietnam War, undoubtedly contributed greatly to Jim Jones' movement.

C. Eric Lincoln and Lawrence H. Mamiya (1980), professors of religion, tell us that Sara Harris studied Father Divine's movement and predicted mass suicide among his followers upon his death. Lincoln and Mamiya suggest that Jim Jones, in his search for information about Father Divine, read this study. They note that Jim Jones, who molded himself after the preaching tradition of black ministers, must have been intrigued by the idea because he made it an intricate part of his cult's practice ritual.

My reference to Father Divine's movement is to illustrate that he drew his membership from a similar kind of underprivileged social class that later supplied recruits to the charismatic Reverend Jim Jones; however, recruitment from lower social economic class is not typical these days because most of today's cultists are not economically underprivileged nor do they come from poor families. Today the surge to cults has had its impetus mainly from the middle class.

Both Father Divine's and Reverend Jim Jones' cult illustrates that illusory beliefs can originate in an intolerable situation, but how does a cult arise when people do not live in such economically desperate conditions in the first place. In order to consider these matters further I will discuss some doomsday cults. These cults attracted middle-class converts. They initiated processes designed to secure evidence to reinforce their millenarian prophecy.

Lake City Cult: When Doomsday Failed

It now is appropriate to consider another historical blueprint for an emerging cult belief system. This time I will illustrate how the basic ideas of cognitive dissonance theory have been applied to a doomsday cult described in *When Prophecy Fails* (Leon Festinger et al., 1956).

Festinger and his colleagues read in a newspaper that Mrs. Marian Keech claimed to be receiving a prophecy from a distant planet that foretold the destruction of the world by a great flood. She claimed that the messages were received through a "magic writing" process, telling her that intellectually superior beings from the planet Clarion had visited earth in flying saucers and forecasted a great flood. Later on she received a message telling that the flood zone would extend from the Arctic Circle to the Gulf of Mexico. Not only did Mrs. Keech learn of the location of the pending doom, but its date was revealed — December 21, 1955.

Festinger and his colleagues decided to test theoretical ideas derived from dissonance theory about what takes place when people hold strong beliefs to which they are publicly committed and then the beliefs become undeniably disconfirmed. Dissonance theory predicted that this inconsistency would produce a state of dissonance arousal and that dissonance, an unpleasant state, would create pressures to bring the person's attitudes and behavior into a relative condition of consistency.

Upon invitation, Festinger's researchers joined Mrs. Keech and her converts two months prior to doomsday and collected data. Festinger observed that Mrs. Keech had gathered around her a small but highly committed group of believers led by a Dr. Armstrong, a physician associated with a university health center.

Between the time Festinger's researchers entered the group and December 21, Mrs. Keech's group continued to receive written messages designed to prepare them for the doomsday ahead. And, even though some of her followers questioned the doomsday prophecy, their resistance and adverse newspaper accounts only helped to strenghthen the beliefs of her faithful followers. Some of Mrs. Keech's followers lost their jobs because of their involvement with the group, whereas other members gave up their jobs and sold their homes as a final preparation.

On December 21, 1955, at 12 AM, the group received word that they were to be picked up by flying saucers in order that they might be saved from destruction. When midnight came, however, and the flying saucers did not arrive, the next few hours were filled with near frenzy and panic. The fatal hour had come, but the saucers and holocaust had not. Then, at 4:45 AM, the group assembled in Mrs. Keech's living room, where she told them that God had spared them — the cataclysm had been postponed. The message that the flood was cancelled because of the group's faith renewed their conviction, and they subsequently continued to proselytize converts. Now what else could Mrs. Keech and her faithful converts do when in point of fact there had been an unequivocal disconfirmation of their doomsday prediction? Of course, they could not deny the cold hard reality of the disconfirmation, or could they? Mrs. Keech could hardly admit that she had experienced a "psychotic reaction," or that the automatic writing telling of the cataclysmic prophecy had in fact been part of her strange delusional system, and, since Mrs. Keech and her cult members had freely chosen to join the group at considerable costs (they were highly committed to the cult's beliefs), the most likely way to reduce dissonance or inconsistency was to seek out additional social support for their religious beliefs; to go out and look for new converts through an all-out effort to proselytize. This in effect is what took place shortly after doomsday had passed and no visitors from outer space called to escort the cult members to the planet Clarion.

Festinger and his associates reasoned that since the prophesized event had not taken place, the cult's belief systems would not be given up easily. But how could the cult resolve the apparent dissonance or inconsistency between their strong commitment to a doomsday belief and the obvious evidence that this belief was indeed disconfirmed? It seemed reasonable to Festinger to conclude that a state of dissonance, established by the disconfirmed expectancy, played the major role in the Lake City cult's vigorous attempt to proselytize new members.

Dissonance theory shows that the failure of a doomsday prediction can have strong motivational properties for those who espouse a millenarian prophecy. Aware of the grim possibilities of doomsday, advocates of doom urge people to set aside worldly feelings and to bind together in time of despair. More recently, Maharaj Ji Houston Astrodome millennium celebration seems like a repeat performance of Mrs. Keech's Lake City cult doomsday fiasco.

Church of the True World: Still Another
Case of Disconfirmed Doomsday

How indeed can one really be sure that when prophecy fails a highly committed cult group's beliefs are always given up? In order to answer this question I will begin again and this time examine a cult who, like Lake City cult, predicted an end of the world. The

cult's prophecy was disconfirmed. They did not, however, pro-
seltize converts.

James A. Hardyck and Marcia Braden (1962) studied a cult group
that splintered off from the Pentecostal Church to make prepara-
tions for a nuclear holocaust.

On July 4, 1960, a group of 103 men, women, and children,
members of the Church of the True World, decended into fallout
shelters to await what they believed would be the final moment of
destruction. All of these people came from the Midwest, gave up
their jobs, sold their homes, and moved to a remote area in the
Southwest to rebuild homes with fallout shelters. All this was in
response to a doomsday prophecy transmitted through their leader
several times and especially on the day that they entered their
shelters: "The Egyptians are coming; get ye to the safe places."

The divine message was received by the cult's members that at
least one-third of the planet Earth's people would be killed by a sudden nuclear attack. The members fully expected to convert the sur-
vivors of the nuclear attack through "divine inspiration." But why
did these cultists believe that a restoration of God could be achieved through a process of paying indemnity for their sins? Prior to the
cult's move to the Southwest, members of the Church of the True
World had engaged in faith healing, speaking in tongues, a call to
conversion, and other prophecies of impending doom. All of this
because the cult members believed that sin and corruption called
for drastic action.

On the day of prophecy, 103 devout cult members went
underground and remained there for forty-two days, anticipating a
nuclear attack, only to find out that six weeks had gone by and the
predicted devastation was not forthcoming. Their beliefs were obviously disconfirmed.

After they emerged from their bomb shelters the group immediately proclaimed that they had passed God's test and now felt
that they were worthy in the eyes of God. They still believed,
however, that a nuclear attack would eventually come. But, in
spite of their unchanged beliefs, none of the cult's members went
back into shelters. What about proselytization? Remember Mrs.
Keech's Lake City cult did proselytize after disconfirmation of
their beliefs. In the case of the Church of the True World, however,

disconfirmation of beliefs resulted in a different distortion of social reality: They contended that a merciful and benevolent God had spared this faithful group from an all-out nuclear attack, and dissonance was reduced. The cult's members felt that there was no need to seek new converts since they had "proven themselves in God's eyes."

Unlike Mrs. Keech's cult, there was little evidence of proselytizing or evidence of publicity seeking following the return to their homes. The group seemed indifferent to attempts of civil defense personnel to talk to them and they turned away curious tourists who wished to inspect their shelters. Obviously these reactions do not confirm dissonance theory, yet the cult's members were as firmly committed to their beliefs as Mrs. Keech's Lake City group.

A comparison of the two doomsday cults—Lake City and Church of the True World—illustrates how dissonance theory can profitably be used to account for a proselytizing reaction to the disconfirmation of doomsday. For example, Hardyck and Braden (1962) note that the Lake City cult had great social support from the cult members and no support from the outside community prior to the proselytizing of new cult members. Too much outside support, according to dissonance theory, would have tended to minimize dissonance, and all but eliminate proselytizing as a mode of dissonance reduction. On the other hand, members of the Church of the True World had isolated themselves from the outside community and there was unanimity for their doomsday belief. Hence, there was little or no need to convince others of their beliefs. On the other hand, the Lake City cult members had experienced great torment and continued outside harassment from their community for their deviant beliefs and practices. Since members of the Church of the True World cult did not need to seek acceptance from their community, they did not serve as a strong source of further dissonance because the community did not attack or criticize them.

My examples of disconfirmed doomsday clearly show how cults react to outmoded and cherished belief systems. To this point, it is obvious that people with strong convictions are hard to change. One might have expected a weakening of beliefs when a plan goes astray but in the case of the Lake City cult the desire to spread the word was quick and resounding. These true believers opened matters for public inspection that were otherwise secret and cherished by the group. This illustrates that beliefs held with deep conviction are not easily shaken or easy to undo. The individual cult believer, however, must have a special kind of group support. It is highly unlikely that a single isolated convert can hold up under disconfirming evidence. All this demonstrates that messianic cults, whatever their place in history, are organized around some future event: the second coming of God or the destruction of the world through a cataclysm; however, only the true believers, according to this prophecy, can be saved.

In order to continue my search for historical insights into how cults are able to attract and convert people into their ranks, I will turn to a third example of a doomsday cult.

The Divine Precepts Believed the End Was Near

Sociologist John Lofland (1966) reports an in-depth analysis of a doomsday cult that flourished on the West Coast during the early 1960s. Lofland labeled the movement the *Divine Precepts* (DP); a pseudonym for Reverend Sun Myung Moon's Unification Church.

According to Lofland's covert research on the Unification Church, DP believed that the world would come to an end and eventually be restored to the Garden of Eden.

The movement's apocalyptic beliefs were originally formulated by Reverend Chang, a Korean, who proclaimed himself Christ of the Second Advent. Ten years after Chang proclaimed himself Christ of the Second Advent, over 5,000 Korean followers were eventually converted to the cult's religion, proclaiming that there would be a restoration of the world to the perfect conditions that once existed. During the early 1960s, at a time when the religious movement had peaked in Korea, Chang's teachings and religious dogma were brought to the United States by a Korean woman, Miss Yoon-Sook Lee.

According to John Lofland (1966), Miss Yoon-Sook Lee was born in Korea in 1918 and converted to Chang's religious movement in 1954. What type of individual was she prior to joining Chang's group? Lofland reports that since her early teens Lee had experienced periods of depression and frequently received visions and heard voices. These "hallucinatory experiences and messianic delusions" finally culminated in a mystical conversion. At this time she decided that her special mission was to do God's sacred work.

Prior to Lee's conversion, she entered a seminary (located in Japan) and studied a variety of religious teachings. After she graduated from the seminary, she refused ordination and subsequently returned to Korea to take a position as a professor of social welfare. Then, after a short teaching career, she enrolled in a Canadian school, ostensibly to further her religious education. During this time she became known as a charismatic religious figure.

Following graduation from the Canadian school, she returned to Korea to take another academic position. She soon suffered from nephritis, however, for which she was unsuccessfully treated by several Korean physicians. After two years of being completely bedridden, Lee lost all hope for cure. As a final act of desperation, Lee was taken to Reverend Chang for a "faith cure." Within a short time Lee appeared to become dramatically cured of her nephritis. As a result of this experience, Lee became totally converted to Reverend Chang's teachings.

Several years after her dramatic conversion, Lee was asked to "go out and spread the word." In order to do this, she left Korea and traveled to the Pacific Northwest coast of the United States in search of converts. However, after two years of hard work she managed to convert only a few faithful members.

The DPs lived, worked, and played together. It was only after great criticism from local newspapers that Lee and her faithful flock left to reestablish their operation in still another city. Shortly after relocating the cult, Lee increased her group's membership to a small number of true believers. Divine Precept members all lived close to Lee and were required to give her all of their money. By this time she had assumed the role of an absolute cult leader. Lee continued to enlist converts for the cause and prepared her flock for what she called the "restoration of a new age."

It remained for sociologists John Lofland and Rodney Stark to explain why DP was able to successfully convert people to the beliefs of this group. For this reason John Lofland, who was asked to join the group, took part in the movement's activities as a participant-observer. For several months Lofland collected some of the most dramatic evidence to date regarding the inner workings of a doomsday cult.

From the results of the DP study, John Lofland and Rodney Stark (1965) identified three predisposing conditions and four situational factors they believe were necessary for total conversion to take place to DP: (a) Members *experienced acute* tension, stemming from a lack of high status and self-worth. These feelings of depression had their origin in an unhappy marriage, job failure, lack of love and acceptance, and, in general, an absence of wholesome relationships with others. (b) Divine Precept members saw the cult as a way to *escape life's problems*, especially medical or psychiatric problems that left many of them in a condition of despair. (c) These *religious seekers labeled themselves true believers or converts* only after conventional forms of religious experience showed little promise or were insufficient to fulfill their deeply felt spiritual needs. (d) A *turning point* took place when the converts became totally involved in and committed to the DP movement. (e) Divine Precept converts *experienced intimate and rewarding relationships* with members who shared a common belief system and values. (f) *Contact* with the *noncult world* gradually decreased, whereas greater attraction to DP increased. (g) As the DP members continued to interact, *commitment* to DP's beliefs and values became more firmly established. This made it increasingly more difficult for extracult influence to modify their views.

Having dissected DP's induction procedures, Lofland and Stark sought to show what motivational factors were at least as important as the group experiences for generating change to DP's doomsday beliefs. They found that only a few of DP members really developed anything like total conversion to the cult's mission or its unconventional religious dogma. In order to develop total conversion, DP converts' religious beliefs and their corresponding religious practices required that they be transformed within a situation psychologists and sociologists label *total environment*. The concept *total environment* refers to groups that create a whole new social community under the assumption that profound and lasting change in beliefs and behavior take dramatic methods to achieve. Total environments are not only situations where modifications in people's behavior take place, but they also remove people entirely from their previous environment in order to create a new one. This is illustrated by what takes place in POW camps as well as cult settings. Here there is complete control over the system of rewards and punishments, and people are taught, through total immersion of the person in the setting, to think and act only in a way deemed proper and correct. This is accomplished through strong pressures (social control) toward conformity and compliance. Reinforcement for appropriate cult-related behavior renders the convert's beliefs more salient and hence more difficult to change through noncult attempts. This is why Lofland and Stark report that DP's total converts had strong behavioral commitments to the cult's practices. Total converts to the Divine Precepts movement were willing to do anything to support the cult's cause. They even rewarded or punished other converts depending on whether they accepted or rejected "divine truth of the cult's doctrine." Proselytizing was a way to demonstrate their total loyalty to the group. After new converts were recruited, they were expected to share DP's belief in the "struggle for redemption and salvation."

In order to promote their religious dogma, DP exploited everyday events that demonstrated an all-pervasive evil was at work as a device for corrupting society: They blamed the devil, what they considered adverse political ideology, like worldwide communism, and/or the moral degeneration of society. It is in this sense that the DP cult represented a form of divine revelation. To this point, DP converts were made by their cult group. Some even experienced an ecstatic feeling or vision that DP's mission was in fact a revitalization in a period of sin and corruption. This is why DP members often recited a litany of heroic religious cult leaders to support their messianic delusions (Lofland, 1966).

Conversion to a "fanatic" religious cult like the DP does not occur as often as it might these days because total commitment to doomsday requires that one surrender one's self and property to the cause. This requires drastic changes in one's lifestyle, beliefs, and behavior. Much more common are the kinds of changes that take place in less exotic cults, requiring lesser degrees of commitment. Nevertheless, the seemingly spontaneous development of events that took place in the DP gives testimony to their attempt to change not only their members but all of society. Moreover, the support that DP had from their total converts created an emotional bond to the point of arousing in members a strong feeling of religious superiority that was apparently effective in changing even the most stubborn neophytes.

The kind of strategy used by the DP is especially important because cults like Reverend Sun Myung Moon's Unification Church have systematically attempted to produce total converts. Reverend Moon's present-day Church draws its converts from college drop-outs. These young people, just as DP's converts, have given up their aspirations for higher education and professional goals to work full time for their newly found religious movement. Just as their predecessors did, they have given up on society and have repudiated the lifestyle of their parents and peers. Their evidence for a new reality is unsuccessfully challenged and guides selectively the kind of information that accommodates their established truths. The more firmly they support their cult beliefs and behavior, the more they become part of a more basic and simple style of life. This is why cult ideology, as I have previously suggested, does not start as a malicious intention to persuade others, but rather it is offered as a more rational way to define social reality and to act on this definition. However, curiously enough, history tells us that the portrait is filled with contradictions so far as the convert's lifestyle and life satisfactions are concerned. All too often the cult dream turns out to be nothing less than a nightmare for many cult members. They seem to suffer the consequences of their idealism simply because the ideal does not exist. Hidden behind the prototype cult or the present-day cult image, we find not only isolated people, but also the potential for ever increasing patterns of dissatisfaction and disillusionment. In order to illustrate this, I will turn to the present-day version of Reverend Moon's Unification Church. Readers will soon discover that they can learn from the Moonies not only that it is possible these days to totally convert people, but also something about the seemingly complex conditions that produce drastic changes in converts who align themselves with a radical cult ideology and its seemingly fanatic religious practices.

Reverend Moon Tells Us That in the End
Only the Good Children Will Be Saved

When one steps out of the rarefied air of the cult group atmosphere and takes a cold hard look at the psychology of cultism, whether one considers Guru Maharaj Ji (the venerable, plump little person who heads up the Divine Light Mission) or the late Reverend Jim Jones of People's Temple, one can easily see why a cultist's beliefs seem to be relatively safe if they are not put to a hard test. That is, inconsistencies can exist for cult members as long as their beliefs and values do not operate on a salient basis or as long as their beliefs are not met directly with strong contradictory experience. This is so because it is now known that people generally use the information that is most available to them or most easily brought to mind when they attempt to define social reality (Tversky and Kahneman, 1974).

In order to gain insight into the workings of a cult, just imagine being in a situation where every minute of each day is programmed (total environment). Each and every day starts with prayer or meditation followed by a simple communal meal and assignment of work duties. Then, the premie goes out into the noncult world to work for the cause: to beg money or sell books or seemingly worthless items. When the cultist returns to the ashram he must listen to a requisite series of spiritual lectures (or Satsangs) delivered by the charismatic guru or one of his staff. This is followed by more prayer and/or intensive meditation. There is no time for the usual leisure. The cult comes first, and all attention is focused on the guru or messiah.

The cult devotee is not allowed to think or read anything not approved by the cult. However, the cultist soon makes an important discovery; there is a handsome payoff for all this hardship and sacrifice: love, acceptance, and a strong emotional bond is formed between the premie and the cult. Finally, the cult's prophet is perceived as supernatural or as an incarnation of God. This experience appears to create a sense of euphoria. This is, no doubt, why all the premie's problems seem to suddenly go away.

Just as with previous cults, the apparent contradiction between what the cultist thinks most people should do and what he actually does is not to be found in the real world but in his dream of utopia. This is why the special sacrifices the young premie has to undergo to gain love and acceptance brings, in the long run, a new identity.

Reverend Moon's cult appeal stems mainly from the all-embracing love (love bombing) and social support his cult offers the homeless and disillusioned "children of the streets." Moon recruits high school and college dropouts. This is not unique because other present-day cults also seek members with similar backgrounds. For instance, David "Moses" Berg (the self-styled Pied Piper) gets his Children of God from young people who at the time have no place else to turn. This is also true of Swami Prabhupada's Hare Krishna and the *avant-garde* rock star Mel Lyman's Brotherhood of the Spirit. Along with the Moonies, these cults seem to share a common delusion about a perfect society.

By the same token, what is known about the membership of the Moon's Unification Church, euphemistically known as the Moonies? There are perhaps about 1 to 2 million members worldwide, with, no doubt, about 10,000 to 30,000 Moonies in the United States. Most of its members are between eighteen and thirty years of age. Moon's "cult children" are required, as is also true of most cults, to surrender to him their worldly goods and personal freedom for the security of the Church. They must relinquish any ties to the outside world. This is so because their minds belong to the cult in exchange for the promise of eternal joy and happiness. Nonetheless, they surrender willingly to the cult because their religion requires that they focus on the cult's leaders. Obedience takes the place of individual expression. The cult offers a sense of belonging and freedom from the everyday stress of competition. All that is asked is energetic proselytizing of other young people on college campuses and street corners. Meanwhile, converts are expected to become subservient to Moon's teachings (Sontag, 1977). On a more theological level, psychologist Daniel Batson (1976) notes that Moon's religion is a strange complex potpourri of orthodox Christianity, dialectic philosophy, anticommunism, and apparent egomania. Nevertheless, Moon's message is clear: "I am a thinker, and I am your brain." His *Divine Prniciple* is based on the premise that people need to be restored to God's divine and sacred grace. Reverend Moon promises to do this for his flock of young devotees.

Philip G. Zimbardo and his associates (1977) contend that a potential convert's initial contact with members of the Unification Church takes place at one of over 125 centers in the United States. Here the perspective convert is confronted with love and acceptance. This all takes place in a familylike setting. The invitation is offered to "do a weekend workshop" where Reverend Moon's teachings can be met head on. However, once the invitation is accepted, there is little time for sleep or for objective self-reflection. Before the weekend is up, the cult requests still further behavioral commitment: a seven-day intensive workshop. This technique, known as *foot-in-the-door*, is familiar to students of social psychology. When a person agrees to a relatively small request, you can then proceed on to an escalation of more extensive requests (Freedman and Fraser, 1966; Pliner et al., 1974; Snyder and Cunningham, 1975). This very same technique has been used extensively in propaganda and consumer advertising programs.

So the critical question is: "What happens next?" We know that the tempo escalates: there are increasing demands made for sacrifice. Little sleep or rest is permitted and potential converts are totally cut off and segregated from family and friends. This is followed by a request for full-time membership. The potential Moonies are told that in order to give more fully of themselves they are required to give up everything and move in to one of the Church's communes. All worldly possessions must go to the Church and full-time membership demands the study of Moon's divine teachings. The premie is also required to solicit funds through a technique known as "heavenly deception." This is where Moonies are asked to say anything to people in order to get them to donate to the Church or to peddle their flowers, candy, or booklets. Premies are also expected to help recruit new members. Males and females are housed apart to assure that "sexual temptation" is kept at a distance. The Unification Church takes care of everything for its members: food, clothing, and "appropriate" marriage partners. This is why Philip Zimbardo suggests that "the Moon cult is not interested in merely influencing attitudes without correlated behavior change" (1977, p. 189).

Although strong devotion and faith may require little or no evidence, most people seem to need some evidence if they are to totally accept the claims made by religious cult leaders like Reverend Moon. The most astonishing thing about the Moonies is that there is a complete absence of any doubt about the correctness of Moon's *Divine Principle.* They never question their faith because Reverend Moon has laid down the precise criteria for how to think and how to feel. He has carefully marshaled and subjected his children to a cool and uncritical appraisal of his dogma; this does not require criticism, only blind faith.

When East Meets West

Although it was fairly easy to document the relationship between some present-day cults and their predecessors, it is much more difficult to determine whether or not there is a link between the wide variety of Indian cults and the more traditional American cult themes. This is because Eastern cults are not essentially an American phenomenon. However, many young Americans have a peculiar eagerness to invest themselves in these new Eastern religions. Actually, it is not a matter of happenstance that most examples of the new Eastern religions presented themselves to young Americans during the 1960s and 1970s. These religious groups have shown an intransigence in the rise of new religious impulses. Suffice it to say that these seemingly highly valued religious movements, among young seekers like the Hare Krishna, took shape when the decisive ingredients in Western religions proved too conventional because of their vestiges of Judeo-Christian tradition. As a result, many young persons have sought the psychospiritual explorations of Indian gurus and Swamis.

There are several variations in Eastern meditation techniques. Nevertheless, meditation is used in many forms of Eastern religions. For instance, the meditative ritual used by the Hare Krishna, the Divine Light Mission, or Transcendental Meditation seems typical of the Eastern forms of cult meditation. In these groups, chanting, mantra meditation, and certain stylized exercises are used to turn the premie's attention away from the distracting affairs of the world. Meditation is employed to rid converts of their sense of guilt and shame and their feeling of inadequacy. The message is clear; the premies can expand their consciousness and they can do this for Lord Krishna as well as themselves.

Today young Americans are seeking out Swami Prabhupada's International Society for Krishna Consciousness. They are looking for a kind of ultimate reality. However, this form of new religion does not propose a real alternative to the American premie's dominant cultural values. Rather Krishnas claim that through deep meditation they will come head on with heretofore neglected realities that in the long run are assumed to enhance the premie's chances for an ultimate state of spiritual bliss. In order to achieve this state, the aging Swami offered his converts the special opportunity to practice the highly valued techniques of Eastern meditation and the chance to leave behind worries of school or work: Krishna takes care of everything.

Who was this Indian Swami who claimed that he could do all this for his faithful followers? Swami Prabhupada contended that he served Lord Krishna, the ancient godhead who is revealed in the Vedic scriptures of Indian philosophy — the *Bhagavad-Gita*. He preached that the present-day world has reached an age of decline and that Krishna chanting and dancing will stave off the inevitable doom. He claimed to have the answer to this seemingly predictable apocalypse; Lord Krishna will appear here on earth to save his most loyal devotees; all others will perish by spiritual forces. This is why Krishnas place themselves above moral law as they go about recruiting the young.

Then, who are these young Krishnas who in recent years have put on saffron robes, shaved their heads, and market the books printed in Krishna-owned printing houses? Many of them were part of the counterculture of the late 1960s. Some of them formerly were exploited by drug pushers before they turned to the Swami's promise of mystical salvation. Some of them are the ex-druggies and ex-potheads who during 1960s turned to Eastern religious meditative techniques as one source of attaining a "natural high" or "mind-expanding experience" as a substitute for the "evils of drug addiction." They now have changed their attire and are part of a group that hopes to shift their consciousness, to reinforce their sense of worth that they claim is connected to a sense of "intrinsic dignity": a self-validating and renewed self-image.

Krishnas are told that if they sell the cult's literature this will raise their level of consciousness. They are also told that it will increase not only their chance for lasting salvation but also the salvation of those who purchase these books.

Hare Krishnas are required to attend temple lectures and worship services. This is where they "set their trap to catch new converts," inviting young idealists to join in the chanting in order to lose their blues. Those who just happen to express a particular interest in Eastern religion and meditation are invited to move into one of the more than fifty temples to undertake the disciplined life of the highly valued Hindu teachings. If recruits accept this offer, they find a highly regimented lifestyle that includes long hours with little sleep, learning about Krishna chanting, meditating, and praying. The new devotees soon learn that everything must be surrendered to the temple. Their shaved heads and their seemingly authentic Indian dress are an expression of their loyalty and devotion to the cult, as is their street begging and peddling of incense, tapes, books, and their own magazine, *Back to Godhead*.

Although certainly not the most celebrated Indian cult, the Divine Light Mission is still another example of an Eastern cult that uses meditation in its stylized ritual. They do not stop there, however. They also employ *satsangs* or a special reinforcement for convert's beliefs. This is done in order to justify meditation and its assumed benefits. Ji encourages the practice of vegetarianism and he stresses celibacy and the abstention from tobacco, drugs, and alcohol as part of the cult's rigorous lifestyle.

Where does the Divine Light Mission get its money? Its members do not sell literature, candy, or flowers like the Moonies and Hare Krishna. The mission gets its money through gifts and from its friends and its members. Premies recruit from their friends and relatives with the promise that they can use meditation to alter their states of consciousness. They even use the technique of placing their tongues to the back of their throat as a way of "tasting true knowledge." There is postdictive evidence suggesting that when this kind of meditation is practiced to excess, people can "bliss out" and care little about themselves or the world in which they live (Cameron, 1973; Singer, 1979).

Guru Maharaj Ji's special religion consists of a potpourri of Eastern and Western scriptures and especially the Hindu teachings found in the *Bhagavad-Gita*. The Guru's premies are expected to learn that he is in fact a messiah much like Jesus, Buddha, or Mohammed. For some of Ji's members, the Guru is God! This chubby little holy person claims to be equal to all gods. Many people believed this until Maharaj Ji took on a lifestyle not in keeping with the usual image of a Guru. Soon his mother, who heads up the Indian counterpart of the Mission, disowned the otherwise "Perfect Master." Nevertheless, the Guru still teaches that God is the omniscient power hidden deep in the consciousness of all people. Ji claims that he and no one else has the key to the knowledge of God's origin. He claims that his devotees are put in touch with God through a strange sort of meditative technique, taught only by the Guru. Maharaj Ji has become independently wealthy and almost 100,000 Americans have received the Guru's knowledge and his blessing as they meditate and read *Divine Times* (a magazine) and *And It Is Divine*, the cult's official publication (Cameron, 1973).

Aside from the usual techniques of meditation, Divine Light Mission has cleaned up its act and has gone after the well educated, the "solid citizens of the community." Today they are living in communal apartments, not as they did formerly in communal houses or ashrams. These are the people who are still enthralled by Guru Maharaj Ji's (Prem Pal Singh Rawat) wisdom.

If Guru Maharaj Ji's psychoreligious explorations take off on a promise of bliss and tranquility, as a substitute for psychedelic splendors and a panacea for all ills, Maharishi Mahesh Yogi's Transcendental Meditation (TM) goes a step further and offers meditation as the ultimate form of mental health. Through this "secret of inner delights" and the realization of a feeling of personal divinity and power, the Yogi sees all human endeavor as a confabulation of the divine. Rumor has it that while in India, Maharishi Mahesh Yogi developed the TM technique only after spending over two years in an Indian cave.

The Yogi's technique entails a process of deep meditation. His people are said to achieve a state of "bliss consciousness." However, when the Yogi attempted to spread the word in India people did not prostrate themselves before the Yogi. This is why he came to the United States, to sell his meditative techniques to a more willing audience. During the early 1960s, the Beatles, Mia Farrow, and the Rolling Stones joined the Yogi. When they left him, the Maharishi dumped his religious jargon and peddled TM as a psychological technique. The movement grew, and by the mid-1970s it claimed a following of 150,000 people and about 6,000 teachers and an annual income in excess of $20 million (Cohen, 1975).

Followers of TM, like followers of Silva Mind Control, claim that it is not a religion, they claim rather that it is a scientific technique used to help people achieve a state of mental relaxation in order to attain their full potential. Nonetheless, the Yogi proposes that the true purpose of life is happiness. This is sought through endless cycles of incarnations and reincarnations because it is felt that only in the human body is there awareness of the true god. To find happiness one must follow the liturgy of the mantra and one must discover "bliss consciousness." In order to achieve this state of bliss, one has only to pay a TM instructor, offer flowers, fruit, a large white handkerchief, assume the lotus position before a picture of the spiritual master, sing a hymn of worship in Sanskrit (the Puja), and receive one's personal mantra for meditation. However, for more cash one can learn an even more elaborate meditative technique used to rid one's self of indifference and everlasting ignorance. Devoted followers at Yogi's TM centers are given the chance to practice the ancient Indian art of levitation. Some of the Yogi's faithful followers believe that through harnessing psychic energy they can raise themselves a foot or two off the floor, and some claim that they can even fly around the room. These gravity-defying feats are said to be the special benefits of "deep and prolonged meditation."

Looking back for a moment at Hare Krishna, Divine Light Mission, and Transcendental Meditation, one can clearly see how these three Eastern spiritual cults seem wretchedly unworthy of offering personal freedom and growth to its followers. This is because their belief systems do not generally support wholesome practices for their disciples. The claim that these are not religious or philosophical movements has proven to be a brilliant marketing ploy; they simultaneously talk about endless cycles of reincarnation and devotees are asked to accept the Guru or Yogi as their personal God. It is known that "bliss consciousness" often turns out to be another way of saying that converts meditate until they reach a state of indifference, where the only thing that seems to matter is devotion to their cult and its Guru.

The format embodied in these Eastern cults is part of a transpersonal paradigm that is much too caught up in the religious benefits of meditation to realize that meditation is also a part of a well-established Asian psychology, where human growth and potential is described in psychological, not metaphysical jargon. For example, Robert Wallace and Herbert Benson (1972) compare TM with biofeedback and they claim that mantra meditation is sometimes beneficial to those who experience the excessive stresses of modern life: It decreases blood flow, oxygen consumption, and produces more "alert brainwave patterns." However, one can accomplish this without supporting Eastern religious beliefs, nor does one have to change his or her lifestyle to fit the ritual of what Eastern cults refer to as an "inner spiritual reality," said to take place through chanting and special forms of prayer.

Finally, it should be emphasized that during the 1960s the religious scene in the United States was in a state of turmoil. During this time there was an appreciable drop in church attendance, an intensification of secular interests, and a growth of the new Eastern religions, attendant upon religious pluralism. America was ripe for these new religions. This trend of secularization and a new religious format followed a relatively long period of modern industrialization. This created the conditions necessary for the development of the Eastern religions as an option to Western religious tradition. This is when the disciples of Eastern religions placed great distance from themselves and traditional religion through their meditative ritual and Hindu discipline.

A New Twist on Science and Religion

For many years, scientific religions have had their share of faithful followers. Christian Science, Theosophy, and, more recently, the Church of Scientology, offer people a strange opportunity to mix metaphors. For instance, Lafayette Ron Hubbard's Church of Scientology claims that scientific methods can be extended into the domain of moral and spiritual concerns. In order to do this, the group uses a *process* to control their converts' thoughts. They intrude on more traditional churches, by standing outside these churches, recruiting the alienated by asking them to join a movement where clear thinking and happiness can be achieved in this lifetime. Scientologists claim that one can gain a special freedom from the death of his or her soul or *theatan*. In order to accomplish this, a state of nirvana is said to be achieved through the study of how *engrams* or *scars* or past bad experiences have become part of the human soul. Through this *process*, converts are encouraged to erase bad memories or *scars* that supposedly took place while the convert was in the fetal stage or even during a previous life. While the convert is *erasing engrams*, his or her physiological responses are measured by what Hubbard calls an E-meter (actually a galvanometer used by psychologists to detect changes in electrical conductivity of, or activity in, the skin). While all this is going on the faithful are encouraged to relive the trauma of their past lives and to free themselves from bad experiences. Scientologists believe that a person's spirit is immortal and that it lives on forever in different bodies, taking different shapes and forms (Garrison, 1974).

The charismatic Hubbard plays to those who accept science, but generally do not understand it, as the solution to their personal and spiritual needs. Many of these people have spent their life's earnings and abandoned their families and jobs as a prerequisite to join Scientology. They have accepted Hubbard's promise of "clear thinking and freedom from bad memories." Hubbard published a book, entitled *Dianetics: The Modern Science of Mental Health*. He has sold thousands of copies through extensive advertising techniques. In this book, L. Ron Hubbard, the science fiction writer and would-be philosopher, has put forth a doctrine that uses scientific language to achieve what he labels "a state of transcendence." Members of Scientology, headquartered in Los Angeles, call each other "brother" and "sister" and they feel a paternal affection for the charismatic Hubbard. Some even confess their most intimate sins to him (engrams).

One might argue that Scientology's appeal verifies the view that some people are confused by the rapid advances in scientific development. Corresponding changes in their value systems have not kept up. These are people who apparently are using religion as an escape from life's dissatisfactions. Yet thousands of Americans are turning to this new theme of materialistic culture, premised upon modern scientific or secular developments; however, most people have managed to avoid scientific cults like the Rosicrucians or the Church of Scientology.

In the final analysis it may be too early to guess what will emerge from this seemingly new scientific cult religious ferment. One would guess that this strange search for truth could lead people to seriously trivialize or ignore the fact that many personal problems are endemic to societal and personal factors, and not owing to past memories or scars. Still the forces that seem to drive people to these movements, no doubt, are a sense of low self-worth and sense of alienation from traditional religion. They search for an identity that has its roots in human strivings for spiritual meaning.

With these considerations in mind, I suggest that Scientology, with its stress on psychological props, is fostered by a strong urge to cast moral and personal problems into the realm of science.

Concluding Remarks

It seems obvious from the preceding historical description of cults and their ever present modern counterparts that most cults are concerned with generating behaviors that compliment a strongly dogmatic version of social reality. This is true even though the lifestyles of religious cultists over the years have varied as much as their charismatic leaders.

Regardless of the historical period, when a cult's members do not privately agree with their cult's practices, they still publicly agree. Regardless of the cult setting, cultists feel a strong obligation to comply. For example, cultists may at first be reluctant to publicly confess sin or to publicly meditate or chant, but when great pressure is brought to bare, they do so. It appears that every cult discussed here has totally converted only a few of its members. Nevertheless, under certain conditions, newly arrived converts comply to a cult's norms more than the cult's total converts (Lofland, 1966; Stoner and Parke, 1978). They follow the ritual of the cult and often protest that they are indeed just as faithful as total converts. This is so because when people voluntarily suffer and endure great hardship for a cause they often show great loyalty to the cause. This is born out by research that shows that the more one chooses to suffer to become a member of a desired group, the more motivated he or she will become to justify the suffering necessary to gain entrance into the group (Aronson and Mills, 1959; Gerard and Mathewson, 1966). There is observational evidence to show that the suffering-dissonance hypothesis suggests that historically those utopian cults who did in fact show signs of "success" required the greatest sacrifices from their members, such as abstaining from alcohol, drugs, the ownership of personal property, and even refusing compensation for hard work (Kiesler, 1978; Kanter, 1972). Sacrifice is a cost and it requires justification. When it comes, this binds members to the cult group.

Over the past three decades many different interpretations have been given to the increase of cults, but they all seem to agree on at least one point: The passage of cult groups from a marginal social phenomenon to a new form of religion has resulted from the steady escalation of frustration and despair and the corresponding growth of an awareness that political ideology and spiritual growth can be translated into action. To those on the outer fringes of society, the message is clear: There must be a renunciation of the outside world. The key person in this drama is the cult leader, whose sacred charge is to deliver his followers from evil, sin, and corruption to an external community of bliss. Despite occasional defection, most members seem sufficiently committed to the cult leader to transfer their loyalties to the cult group and remain in the fold. This calls for intense levels of sacrifice because most people would not surrender their personal freedom and burden the cult prophet with the responsibility of making decisions for them.

One might suspect that the changes required for cult membership are not easy adjustments to make in a person's life, despite the seeming legitimacy of the cult group's shared religious beliefs and practices. But cults do not encourage self-criticism and doubt seems almost nonexistent; nothing seems open to question. The problem with cults is not just their curtailment of the individual's freedom of choice, for such does not exist where people seem to be happy when they are led by a charismatic leader, but instead the seeming righteousness of their religious cause and the godlike illuminations they attribute to their leader that only in the long run enhances the convert's frustrations. This is why cultists can become increasingly disdained. Despite grim historical litany of opposition to cults, this only makes their struggle all the more worthy in the eyes of their members. In the condition of social isolation and continued outside rejection, some cults can become increasingly "extreme" or "fanatic." This was no less true of past cults then it is of present-day cults.

In the next chapter I will be concerned with cult leaders. I turn to this topic because in order to understand how a cult messiah or guru is able to bring about anything like total obedience or conformity to his or her cult's religious practices, it must first be understood why people form cult groups, how they select a particular cult to join, and how the cult leader organizes the group cultists belong to. When one turns to the topic of cult leaders one finds that one of the most perplexing and seemingly perennial puzzles is how to explain charismatic religious cult leadership.

The singlemindedness that characterize cult leaders, while considered necessary by converts to ensure the growth of their cult, can turn into a liability if the cult faces a crisis. When this happens the cult leader often is characterized as a fanatic, a messiah or guru with a one-track mind who views everything in strict cult survival terms: a leader who has a fixed idea that all that is corrupt and evil about society flows from forces outside the cult. Since a crisis is a situation where something must be done in a hurry to prevent or at least delay the consequences, the prophet must act immediately. This is the tragedy and often the downfall of some cult leaders; Jim Jones, for example. This is why one would do well to seek the wisdom of George Santayana's well-known adage: "Those who cannot remember the past are condemned to repeat it."

5

Cult Leaders, Charisma, and True Believers

Cult Leaders and Their Followers

The behavior of cult leaders is, of course, determined by many factors. For instance, the group conditions, such as isolation from the general community and social support for the leader's beliefs, often influence what the cult messiah or guru does. Under authoritarian conditions, the cult leader determines the group's goals and gives step-by-step orders so that members are certain about their future. There is evidence that leaders who enjoy the unanimous support of their followers make risker decisions for their group than those who lack such support (Clark and Sechrest, 1976). Then, as you might expect, this kind of cult leadership has a marked effect on the behavior of the group's members.

Nonetheless, some leaders scrutinize their followers very closely; others seem to allow their converts more autonomy. This is why we must condider the conditions that favor charismatic and author-itarian styles of leadership. Under these conditions, where people have experienced highly stressful circumstances, they may be more acceptable of autocratic leadership.

Identifying with and acquiescing to a cult guru's or messiah's demands can, no doubt, best be understood if one realizes that many religious seekers seem to lack a sense of personal worth.

They often join a cult out of a strong desire to become part of their leader's plan for a more meaningful religious experience. When this happens their personal judgment can become subjected to the autocratic leader's ability to sway and persuade them to give up on their family and belongings with the promise of eventually reaching a "state of higher consciousness" (Singer, 1979). Obviously, then, the absolute power of the leader is an important factor that needs consideration.

Exhorted by a cult messiah or guru, cult people can be triggered to an obedience of his or her ritual and practice. This is because most cult leaders have gained their status and achieved acceptance by their followers through their special talent to influence them. In contrast, conventional leadership in most day-to-day situations tends to fall to those who best exemplify the already existing norms and values of the group, whereas leadership in cults falls to the person who has imposed his values and beliefs on those who are enthralled by his teachings. Some divinity scholars have observed that people who submit to the absolute authority of a religious leader seem capable of submitting to the dogmatic ideal of the autocratic leadership of the cult leader (Needleman and Baker, 1978). Does this suggest that people who hold dogmatic religious beliefs can be more easily influenced by the highly emotional appeal of a cult leader than those who do not, especially when the would-be prophet attempts to elicit from them a reawakening of a born again conversion? There is evidence that shows that it is difficult for dogmatic religious seekers (or true believers) to seriously resist this "divine message" (Cohen, 1975). However, generalizations from these findings are difficult to make because religious seekers vary in their characteristics just as religious cult leaders vary in their leadership style.

So we are left with the conclusion that, following a religious conversion, dramatic alterations have taken place in most converts, and these changes are due to the powerful influence of a charismatic religious figure. But, are these changes more or less permanent or at best only temporary? Many people who are "converted" eventually return to their family and revert to their original beliefs. Some even attempt to repudiate their former cult's leader's doctrine (Cohen, 1975; Stoner and Parke, 1978). This is precisely where the difficulties lie for the cult leaders: he or she may come to play only a minor role in providing the special kind of social support and spiritual awakening his followers are seeking. Even if this is true, it can be argued that a cult leader's ideology and religious dogma can be a threat to socially acceptable self-standards for religious beliefs and practices.

Following from this logic, the cult leader's beliefs, even if only temporarily adopted, can erode feelings of individual responsibility or standards for self-control because these cannot develop when the person's behavior and religious beliefs are programmed. This is because religious cult leaders generally call for only blind veneration and absolute obedience from their followers. This is why the cult setting encourages a "blood and guts" approach to problem solving, where denigration of reason is common and "intellect takes a back seat." Rational thinking, in a more conventional sense, and intellect are likely to be considered a source of evil, or the devil's work (Doress and Porter, 1978).

There are strong indications that people who become converted to a cult religion are dehumanized as leaders attack their beliefs and behavior. Finally, the person may give up his or her strivings for personal control and freedom (Singer, 1979). This is likely to happen because the cult group and its leader use strong persuasive measures to bring about uniformity of behavior, and, of course, this operates against the individual's more rational forms of judgment. The rigid conformity to a cult lifestyle, as required by the cult leader, becomes the norm or the accepted mode and is likely to be viewed as a form of deviancy from the perspective of the noncult world. To this point, I have described the potential cult convert as one who is recruited into the cult and eventually accepts the cult's beliefs and values. I now turn to a more detailed examination of how cult leaders can call for total loyalty and absolute obedience from their followers.

As I have previously indicated, it is sometimes difficult to ascertain just exactly what makes a person join a cult, but whatever the reasons, the morass of cult participation and indulgence can indeed pressure the member into more than casual participation. And as I have already suggested, one source of common concern to psychologists is that, for some persons, a cult group identity can be so firmly established that the member will experience a dramatic change in his or her beliefs and lifestyle. Indeed, there is good reason to believe that it is loyalty to the cult group leader that renders the convert's capacity to function in the noncult world less likely (Singer, 1979). The assumption here is that many cult members seem to believe that loyalty to their religious leader is somehow a higher form of truth than the benighted views of their traditionally religious parents of the noncult world. They claim that traditionalists have contributed only spiritual confusion and chaos to the world. This suggests that if the thrust of seminal traditional religious thinkers denounce this "new shift in consciousness," the faithful disciples of cult leaders then claim ultimately to seek an "enlightened consciousness" by following more vigorously the prescribed discipline of their cult.

Strict *cult morality*, examples of which include drugs and alcohol abstinence, is closely linked to the cult leader's special dogmatic religious teachings. There seems to be a marked positive correlation between a member's loyalty to the cult's religious practices and his or her inability to function in the cult as an independent thinking individual. I suspect that in some cases this special brand of *cult morality* is purposely designed by the cult leader to control members (Cohen, 1975).

The Judeo-Christian tradition teaches that faith is a divinely ordained union of the individual with God. Most contemporary religious cults teach that a deepening of commitment to the cult and its leader comes first. Cultists claim that commitment to their cult is supposed to lead to a new and deepened understanding of the self. This is characterized by an assumed *intuitive* or *spiritual feeling*. Some converts claim that reason and intellect had little to do with their cult conversion or with the development of their new cult-derived identity (Needleman and Baker, 1978). Recent research suggests that the greater the convert's sense of subjective religious experience, the greater his or her overall religious view of the world (Hood, 1975), and, the greater a convert's religious orientation to problem solving, the greater his or her expressed purpose in life (Bolt, 1975; Soderstrom and Wright, 1977). This is what has been labeled *a new motive and purpose for living* (Paloutzian, 1976). Actually, there is evidence supporting this view because "born again" converts internalize their cult's religious beliefs and they even act upon them. That is, converts live in accordance with their cult's religious precepts (Paloutzian et al., 1978).

Implicit in a cult leader's religious dogma is the view that cult members can create a new and more rewarding society that does not make the same kind of demands on cultists as they experienced before joining their cult. They believe that this is possible because they have severed themselves from mainstream religion. Their cult represents a strong reaction against more established religious groups. This is why cultists perceive themselves as unwilling to compromise their leader's religious beliefs. This is necessary in order to survive in a religious setting that requires total commitment to the cult leader's plan for utopia.

The apparent cult-mainstream religion dichotomy increases a convert's faith in the cult leader's teachings. It also tends to superordinate all other lesser motives because converts believe that their messiah or guru will create for them a new and more perfect society — the ultimate utopia. This cult utopia is an attempt to construct an ideal society and it is the product of the messiah's or guru's "strange brand of fantasy." Seldom is the leader's plan a reasonable or more rational alternative because it does not fit the demands of people who live in a complex modern society. However, true believers are ready for it because they claim that they can no longer live in what they consider a disintegrating society. The supporting beliefs of cult members for this view provides further confirming evidence for the cult leader's teachings. This is why there usually exists a high consensus among cult members that indeed the greater society is "sick." This apparent group consensus provides religious seekers with the rationale for defending their dream of a perfect society. However, to the extent that the cult leader's utopian beliefs are seemingly untestable, the challenge of a perfect life seems at least demonstrated in principle. There are good reasons for this because one of the most powerful agents of influence used by a cult leader is his or her focus on the possibility of a better life for all of the cult's members. This belief, as I have already suggested, can lead young cultists to seek the ultimate utopia. There is an amazing twist to this story, the convert becomes more convinced than ever before that the leader is right. The messiah's or guru's message becomes more appealing as the convert's world seems to fail. Disciples suddenly become more interested in not only convincing themselves of the validity of their leader's cult utopia, but in also convincing others of the correctness of this dream. No matter what the evidence, convincing others to join the cult group is a way of adding additional evidence that their leader is right. In most cases, too, the kind of cult leader that emerges is one that has only special meaning to the followers. He or she is likely to play down conflict and disagreement in the group and to highlight conflict in the greater society. For example, many of the new religious leaders, like Guru Maharaj Ji and Swami Prabhupada, adopted positions that renounced Western society as they began to catch the attention of young Americans who wanted an alternative to drugs. Without their charismatic leaders, cults like the Divine Light Mission or the Hare Krishna would find it difficult to exist.

The reason why a cult group can rise to its pinnacle is because the greater society provides the motivation to view itself as "sick" and "corrupted." Yet, even within the limits set by a cult's vision of utopia, not all members are completely convinced nor do they totally accept their cult leader's fantasy. Then, behind the cult leader's throne, there are some examples of disbelief and dissatisfaction with the cult's ideal. Nevertheless, whether or not a convert totally yields to the vision of the charismatic cult leader, the potential for influence is greater when the convert underestimates his or her capacity to be influenced or to resist. It is not just a matter of what the convert is told; it depends, to a large part, on how persuasive and how credible the message is and how vulnerable the person is to the leader's power to influence (Roof, 1978).

In contrast to a sense of helplessness and alienation that characterized the cultist's precult life, there is a *new sense of optimism* and a newly discovered efficacy that accompanies the member's sharing of the cult leader's dream for utopia. I propose that this is the case because the cult's efforts to achieve a purpose in life has driven many faithful converts to the cult leader in the first place. When premies take this kind of action, it can make them feel accepted and loved; it is equally plausible that they are protecting themselves from the realization of their feelings of failure, helplessness, despair, and apathy. All in all, many cultists are dissatisfied persons who are motivated to rid themselves of feelings of low-self worth. This assumption is borne out in recent research done with ex-cultists (Singer, 1979).

Margaret Thaler Singer (1979), in an unstructured interview, talked with about 300 ex-cultists. She also obtained background information on them and found that a large portion of them did not know why they joined a cult. There was an overall tendency for these young people to blame themselves, especially if they had a negative cult experience. A large number of Singer's subjects told her that their precult life was characterized by despair and anxiety.

Obviously, from Singer's research, it can be concluded that cultists become increasingly more self-blaming as they place some distance between their former cult and themselves. But, for the most part, they still remember, and they still hold strong feelings of affection for their former cult friends.

All of these factors, Singer discovered, clearly suggest a perennial theme characteristic of the ex-cultist: The more the cult leader required great sacrifice (abstinence and austerity), the more difficult it was for the young person to renounce his or her former cult leader. One of Singer's most interesting findings was that the communal sharing and acceptance of the convert, the essence of cults, was related to the survival of the cult group. For a while, at least, the cult leader did succeed in providing the former convert with an abundance of seemingly accessible goals; this was accomplished at the cost of the person's feelings of personal autonomy, however. This pattern held true for Singer's ex-cultists because they were required to surrender to the strict ideological and religious demands of their cult group and its leader. It is important to note, however, that the rigid authoritarian leadership of the cult messiah managed to prove too restrictive for those who left the cult of their own accord.

Of great psychological interest here is the question of how people reach a state where they conclude that they are totally committed and dependent on their cult messiah. A number of explanations have been proposed to account for this process; however, there is convincing evidence suggesting that when people attempt to understand the causes for others' behavior (or one's own behavior), they either overestimate the influence of personality traits or situational factors. Social psychologist Lee Ross labels this process "the fundamental attribution error" (Ross, 1977, p. 184). For example, it seems highly unlikely that most people would consider the prospect of a cult membership — "it only happens to other people." Recent psychological research strongly supports the view that people are not generally aware of how others have influenced their beliefs and their behavior, however (Nisbett and Wilson, 1977). Nonetheless, if you observe a Hare Krishna selling books, it seems to help you to understand what is going on if you can assume that the cultist in question is "just plain crazy." However, if you find out that the Krishna appears to be genuinely kind and loving, you cannot understand this action unless it can be attributed to the cult group. The reaction is: "they program the premie to appear loving and kind in order to sell the cult's books or to recruit cult members." In other words, when people cannot find a powerful situational explanation for a person's seemingly strange behavior, they are likely to infer that there is something about the person that makes him behave strangely. What I am suggesting here is that there may be a tendency for most noncultists to attribute the cause of a cultist's "fanatic" behavior to personal *dispositions*; people are likely to assume that there is something wrong with cult people; they may reason that young cultists possess certain negative traits that cause them to act the way they do. On the other hand, the cultist is likely to explain his religiously oriented behavior in *environmental* or *situational* terms, as if to say "the cult made me do it" (Frieze and Bar-Tal, 1979).

Ironically, there is strong psychological evidence that people act on the information they have available to them. When people do this they have a tendency to overestimate the importance of nature over nurture as determinants of behavior. This *egocentric-attributional bias* results in people assuming that negative behavior is caused by negative traits rather than consider that membership in a particular religious group, like an exotic cult, can produce what is labeled *deviant behavior* (Ross, 1977). Following a similar line of reasoning, it has been observed, not surprisingly, that cultists tend to use their cult group and the actions of their cult leader as a basis for defining social reality. Hence, when the member does not conform to the cult's standards other cult members feel uncomfortable because nonconformity tends to disrupt the cult's basis for social comparison and threatens the accomplishment of their shared goals.

It is easy to understand why conformity and an intense sense of involvement and commitment to the cult's standards are required of all cult members. Hour after hour, and day after day, cult converts must show that they care and accept and love each other. The premies soon learn to cope with the continual emotional demand of "love bombing" and eventually develop an intense sense of commitment to the cult group and its leader. For instance, Margaret Thaler Singer (1979) tells us that many former cultists report that before they could perform their cult role effectively, they had to learn to love and accept their "brothers and sisters," whereas they were required to detach themselves completely from the greater society and especially from their family and former friends. They come to view the goals of their cult leader as absolute and binding. In other words, all too often cultists are locked into their cult role because they have duties and special obligations that must be met regardless of what they at first feel is right or correct or believe is fair and just.

I am not claiming that all of the new religions have members who experience what I have been describing. But I do believe — and my knowledge of cults has tended to support this — that a certain percentage of cult members feel uncomfortable with how their lifestyle fits into their cult leader's plans for their salvation. Fortunately, this situation does not fit all of the new religious movements because this is changing; some groups have attempted to make their members realize that they must work on their personal problems. In such cases this is an individual process and not related to the group's goals. Not only that, but some new religious leaders, like those who run the Neighborhood Foundation's Zen Center, serve as examples of what these new religious groups can do for their members. For example, groups like the Zen Center have sought to create more wholesome lifestyles for their followers than the Hare Krishna or the Divine Light Mission.

Sadly enough, in spite of what I have said, values prescribed by a cult leader can replace the individual member's values; loyalty to the cult group and its leader can supersede the individual's values. Even when cultists protest that they should not comply to the cult's standards, they eventually go ahead and do what they are told even when, under different circumstances, dissent might dramatically underscore their bahavior. They remain instrumental to the purpose of the cult and they act as if their cult leader's requirements are a means to an end. All this takes place when there is an attempt to maintain the cult's status quo and when the cult leader demands complete obedience from the followers.

It seems that those who work for the cult's cause rarely, if ever, come to understand why they "give all" to the cult because there seems to be more than sufficient justification to perform what is expected. Not only does loyalty and hard work for the cult's cause seem reasonable, it is also absolutely necessary. Here is the paradox of cult membership — the same people who can commit themselves to a cult can easily distort reality and rationalize their cult leader's behavior according to acceptable cult norms. In such cases, it can be strongly argued that cultists are just responding to the intense situational pressures that seem to determine their behavior. In the rational analysis that social distance from the cult scene provides people who live in the noncult world, it is easier for people to believe that cultists are "crazy" or "possessed of some demonic force" rather than realize that cultists are conforming to the standards set for them by their charismatic cult leader (Jones and Nisbett, 1971).

What general conclusions can I draw from my analysis of cult-related practices? First, cultists perform their duties and obey their cult master not so much because they possess certain personality traits, but mainly because of the intense situation confronting them. Cultists are idealists who just happen to find themselves in a desperate situation. Second, in line with this reasoning, one of the most consistent research findings on social influence is that people use the salient features of their environment to define social reality. Taken in this sense, the standards of the cult leader operate to define what is proper and correct for his cult's members (Taylor and Fiske, 1978).

The Emergence of Cult Leaders

In preceeding chapters, I discussed the seemingly puzzling phenomena of the widespread attraction of exotic religious cults in America. I now turn to an examination of the potential harm to converts when they turn away from family, school, and work to dedicate themselves wholeheartedly to an autocratic cult leader. But if religious cult leaders are to have great influence on their followers, converts must also be influenced by their peers. This happens in their daily living conditions and when they go out together to proselytize for their cult. Probably the most important result from this strong commitment to their cult leader and their peers is that it all pays off: They come to accept their leader's promise for a better life. Nevertheless, ideological or religious factors are not always as significant to the premie as is the hope for greater self-fulfillment.

In this section I will examine the characteristics of the cult leader. I will suggest how certain leadership qualities, along with the constraining cult environment, can produce the kind of grandiosity associated with charismatic cult leadership.

"Radical" groups can hold a conviction that their leader is the *raison d'être*. This is why members of "radical" groups come to believe that the group's very existence would not have taken place without their leader's presence. Anyone who has observed cult leadership in operation could easily identify why one individual and not another is the cult's charismatic leader. What do psychologists mean by cult leadership? According to Edwin P. Hollander, all forms of leadership entail at least three different factors: (a) a leader whose attributes are focused on the group's goals; (b) followers whose attributes are relevant to the group situation; and (c) a particular situation where a leader-follower relationship can emerge (Hollander, 1976). It is in this context that the leader typically obtains status, recognition, and other social reinforcements for moving the cult group toward its expressed goals. However, this is not the whole story because followers obtain social and personal reinforcement when they achieve their goals in consort. Hence, the relationship between a leader and followers involves an exchange of reinforcement where both benefit from the relationship, but not without costs in time and resources to both (Homans, 1974; Mackenzie, 1978). For example, when cult members accept the guru's or messiah's religious dogma, the acceptance stems from the strong logical argument the cult leader expounds. The cost to converts is dependency on the leader, whereas the leader may create resentment and resistance from the followers.

That is, the cult leader may first encounter opposition from the converts, but when they show a willingness to accept the hard work required of them, the messiah may encourage them, with great equanimity, to express their true feelings. If converts indicate to the leader that everything he or she says will be subjected to the cold glance of logic, and that he or she will be judged accordingly, a barricade may be thrown up between the cult leader and the converts. In this case, it would be pointless for converts to pursue a line of dissent, since it would fall on a closed mind, if not deaf ears. Premies need to make the messiah aware that they are not resisting, that there are perhaps even elements of irrationality behind the converts' opposition to the cult leader. Then, no matter how sound the converts' arguments seem, they can't have a decisive effect, even if they are placed in opposition to the cult leader's dogma. The cult leader's beliefs and values have greater merit. When this happens, converts lose and the cult leader wins, and both have suffered costs. The cult leader's status has been challenged and the premies' self-esteem, no doubt, has been lowered. This renders converts increasingly more dependent on the cult's messiah. In time converts are likely to doubt their own ability to reason and think independently of the cult leader's established dogma (Rice, 1976).

There is unequivocal evidence that suggests that most effective leaders (including religious cult leaders) tend to assume responsibility for their followers' lives. They attempt to maintain and establish credibility with them so that responsibility is obvious. The leader must also encourage members to assume personal responsibility for the accomplishment of the group's goals. This is why a cult leader must establish credibility as a viable religious leader without at the same time reducing the commitment of the converts to the cult's stated objectives (Jabes, 1978).

All leadership focuses primarily on the processes of social influence. A widely accepted definition of a leader is one who exerts "great influence" on the actions of his followers (Fiedler, 1971). The idea here is that a leader has the power to produce group-based behavior in what is taken as the "desired direction." Autocratic leadership requires that people follow the leader's suggestions or orders without question. This definiton of leadership proposed here certainly fits cult leaders. Similarly, there is little by way of group resistance that might prevent subordinated premies from expressing different views from those of the cult leader. Then, to avoid the torment of making decisions about their lives, converts acquiesce to the programming of events set for them by the autocratic cult leader. However, when converts give in to the demands of their cult leader there is no feeling of having made a mistake because, at this time, there is a feeling that all is well. All too often converts are inclined to feel that they have done the best that they could with their lives. Instead of suffering the hardships of decision making, converts seem to have improved their potential for a better and more fulfilling life. And, as long as the converts do not undergo a lag or setback, all of their troubles seem to go away (Bellah, 1967).

But what are the bases of a cult leader's power? A key aspect is that, since the cult setting is a bedrock of conformity and obedience, many cultists share one common ingredient — their acceptance of their leader's stringent rules governing their lives. When it comes to matters of "proper behavior" and "correct thinking" — how and what to believe — these young religious seekers often defer to the dogmatic beliefs of their cult leader. Consequently, devotees of cults, like the Hare Krishna and the Unification Church, are taught exclusively from prayer books and scripture texts written by their leaders. Knowledge of these works are used to create conformity to the actions and beliefs of the cult. Hence, the change in the young premie's acceptance of the leader's beliefs can be gradual or sudden, but when the convert starts to accept the guru or cult messiah it becomes obvious where the basis of power lies.

On a more specific level, French and Raven (1959) have identified five sources of social power leaders use to control their followers: (a) *Reward power* is based on the leader's ability to reward members of the group. In this sense, cult leaders dispense social rewards within their group, such as praise and acceptance of those who are singularly disillusioned and dissatisfied with their life. (b) *Coercive power* is based on the leader's ability to punish members of the group for violations of the cult's norms. For example, a cult leader can generally punish followers for deviations from the group's standards, and still retain their respect and love. (c) *Expert power* relates to the leader's expertise on matters of importance to the group. Cult leaders devise their cult's ideology and religious practices, and they are the main interpreters of the group's goals and values. To this point, predictably, the cult's members rally beyond their authoritarian leader. Instead of relying on principles of internal control, converts are oriented to the external standards of their cult master. This seems necessary because too much disagreement with the cult leader can "bring the whole house down." (d) *Referent power* is based on a follower's desire to identify with the leader. Most cult followers seem to idolize their leader, and they generally internalize their leader's values. Some cult followers think that their cult leader is God, or at least one who has supernatural powers. (e) *Legitimate power* is based upon the leader's belief that he or she has a divine right to control the lives of the followers. In this case, cult group followers believe that their leader has a divine right and duty to demand obedience from them and they seem more than willing to comply.

If cult leadership is the ability of an individual to influence others, then followers, to a certain extent, are influenced because they see it as being in their best interest. Even in groups less structured and less formal than cult groups; therapy group, for example, some people are more likely than others to be in close contact with the group's leader, depending on their position in the group. At group therapy sessions, group members are provided with a setting where they are strongly encouraged to fully disclose their feelings about others as well as their feelings toward themselves. The "leader" of a therapy group, much like the cult leader, often deals with people who have serious psychological or medical problems. Unlike the group cult leader, the therapist is not likely to employ faith healing techniques as a means to establish credibility. However, an analysis of the procedures employed by cult leaders and group therapists suggests that they share certain similarities, regardless of their training or discipline differences. For example, there is a positive relationship between how the group "therapist" and the cult leader attempt to convince their respective groups of their leadership qualifications. In both cases the leader must show empathy for others' feelings and demonstrate leadership expertise (Truax and Charkhuff, 1967). As a matter of fact, psychiatrist Louis Rose (1970), who has been investigating the claims and practices of charismatic faith healers for many years, has attempted to show that these would-be miraculous cures are related to converts' beliefs in prophecy, magic, and acceptance of the leader's strong religious beliefs. Rose presents evidence showing that religious faith healing is by and large the result of *suggestion* used as a therapeutic agent under conditions of high emotional arousal.

Psychiatric disorders are often alleviated through faith healing, even though little or no empirical evidence supports the view that faith healers are the miracle workers they claim. As a matter of fact, Rose failed to find one miracle cure that could stand up to careful empirical scrutiny. In spite of this observation, when a cultist believes that his cult leader possess a special ability to cure people, this requires little or no direct evidence because most cultists accept their leader's claim; they do not even begin to question their cult messiah's alledged divine talents. The prayers and exhortations of the cult faith healer are taken as if emanating from an oracle or prophet.

Cult Leaders: A Special Case of Charisma

Cult leaders are *charismatic* because they are perceived by their followers as having *divine power* and a special calling. For example, Charles Manson, Jim Jones, Reverend Moon, David "Moses" Berg, L. Ron Hubbard, Swami Prabhupada, Guru Maharaj Ji, Love Israel (Paul Erdman), Maharishi Mahesh Yogi, Jimmie Roberts (Brother Evangelist), and countless other cult leaders, although widely different in their leadership style, have been able to inspire confidence and to obtain great sacrifice from their cult devotees (Bird, 1978). Nevertheless, a prototype of the charismatic cult leader is difficult to discover. According to Louise Rose (1970), historically the charismatic faith healer, from the primitive medicine man to modern cultist, testifies to the aura and powerful impact faith healers can have on their faithful followers. However, at first glance, it appears that charismatic cult leaders are those who are able to induce their followers to perform extraordinary behavior; however, charismatic cult leaders tend to be self-flattering. They often attempt to convince their converts that only they have the mystic power to induce a special religious conversion and to lead followers to utopia (Rice, 1976). For example, charismatic cult leaders are often able to assure potential converts that they can all be saved — which means a promise of everlasting salvation and tranquility to the potential devotee. As the drama proceeds, the charismatic messiah produces an outcome for his or her followers not unlike that of hypnotic suggestion used by the familiar stage hypnotist (Rose, 1970). The reputation of the cult leader's greatness does not stop there, however, it even includes the claim of a miraculous birth and precocious childhood. Even would-be scoffers find themselves influenced when in the presence of a charismatic cult leader like Reverend Moon (Zimbardo et al., 1977).

It is no accident, then, that charismatic religious leaders seem to provide followers with impressive evidence of their "divine characteristics." Their success as leaders is difficult to explain fully, however. For example, Tucker (1968) found that cult leaders inspire people to accept them because of love and passionate devotion. He suggests that some kind of acute distress seems to predispose people to perceive their cult leader as one who offers a special kind of salvation and redemption, especially for those who just happen to be enthusiastically faithful followers of the leader.

By virtue of the leader's unusual attributes (credibility factors), and ability to promise hope and everlasting salvation, cult followers are likely to conclude that they will be delivered by their cult leader to the "promised land" because their leader is assumed to possess the necessary and sufficient "messianic attributes" to do so (Weber, 1947).

In situations where the members of the group feel emotionally dependent on their leader, the cult leader can assume a charismatic role. But first he or she must appear to have a strong sense of mission; a strong belief that he or she has the ability to change society; and a feeling that he or she is destined by God to protect others from sin and corruption. The cult leader must also exhibit high self-confidence and inspire people to follow him or her in pursuit of a more positive self-image. This kind of religious leader must also focus on reducing distress and disillusionment for followers. These seem to be the minimum requisites for charismatic leadership.

Since charismatic leaders claim that they possess special talents ("supernatural powers"), they are the antithesis of democratic leaders. Charismatic leadership is often unstable, however, because leaders who rely on their charisma constantly have to prove themselves: They must demonstrate that they possess the special talents or powers they claim. As a matter of necessity, the leader must stabilize the cult's ritual and make members' role expectations clear.

An established charismatic leader is closely scrutinized by the followers. This makes it necessary to prevent the cold hard contradictions of the myth from becoming obvious to the converts. This is why Max Weber contends that charismatic leaders tend to routinize their power. In this regard, there is evidence that most cult leaders manage to do this through special techniques, for example, faith healing, to establish credibility with their followers (Sontag, 1977).

A cult leader's claim of charisma is likely to perpetuate an unfortunate misconception because followers stubbornly refuse to challenge their leader's "divine right" to offer salvation. Converts love and worship their messiah or guru. Why not, when they have been promised everlasting salvation and have little reason to doubt their leader's claim. An understanding of this conception of leadership is especially important because it illustrates what I mean by charismatic cult leadership.

Anyone who has ever watched an exotic cult leader knows full well that his or her act is part of an "idiosyncratic cover story." The cult leader typically assures potential converts (and total converts) that he or she will put them in touch with, and let them experience, God firsthand. Observers are sometimes reduced to a childlike dependence on the cult leader. Unbeknownst to the potential convert, the charismatic has produced the initial stage for cult conversion. However, under most everyday circumstances, without the powerful influence of the cult leader, it is doubtful whether a cult conversion for most would ever take place.

How great and lasting is the power of the charismatic leader? After people have been converted to a cult, they eventually come to believe it is their special duty, and even their supreme obligation, to obey their "cult master's" demands. When a cult leader, like Reverend Jim Jones, isolates followers from the outside world, these desperate conditins can be used by the leader to validate the claim that he is indeed the leader of his followers' choice. In such cases, cult converts, like those found in People's Temple, can be asked to experience martyrdom first hand, rather than read about it in sacred texts. We might do well to remember this potential for fanatism and self-destruction.

As complex as the issue of cult leadership is, some patterns in profile of the religious cult leader emerge. This is true because there are certain factors in the religious beliefs of cult members that work against outright disobedience to their leader. The leader has the power to promise a better life for cult members. This proposition rests with the perception that the cult leader has "divine authority," which followers believe to be true. Converts believe that their leader has the power to hasten or to even retard the emergence of their salvation because they seem to believe that this cannot come to pass without their charismatic leader's plan.

Even if a cult leader does not promise "everlasting salvation" for converts, the leader instills a sense of dedication to the cult's cause. As a result, the cultists develop an all-embracing special purpose in life; they can even come to face death. Everything the convert believes, and every deed performed by the convert, is a special kind of sacrifice for a noble cause. Cult followers seem driven to spare nothing for their cult master because their aim is to find a better life though their special religious experience. So it is that cult followers seem to live in expectation of an imminent and total redemption, yet their beliefs cannot be translated into action without their charismatic leader. This is true because they believe redemption and the better life that promises to ensue can only be achieved by a special messiah, like David "Moses" Berg, who takes on the mission of saving followers from everlasting sin and great personal torment. It is in this sense that the cult leader is perceived as the mediator between what is taken as supernatural and a special kind of cult reality. This is why the cult leader represents a divine prophet; he or she is the "messianic incarnation of God."

The cult leader is assumed to possess a special kind of power (credibility); the power to supply followers with a sacred exegesis when all other hope and promise is gone. When we look for the basis of a cult leader's authority we find it in the loyalty and absolute obedience of the faithful converts. In the final analysis, the revelatory basis for cult leadership is the belief that a prophet has a legitimate claim to divine authority, and followers are inspired to obey and to follow their messiah. Then, to the followers, the cult leader is a god whose power they can take into themselves merely by loving and giving their complete and absolute approval. To do anything else would divert the cult's mission that was designed by the cult leader in the first place (Cohen, 1975).

The Search for a Cult-Leader Personality Type

One common illusion about cult leaders is that there are certain negative personality characteristics associated with their leadership style (Cox, 1978). We are thus led to a rather ironic conclusion: it appears that the more a cult leader uses coercive and deceptive tactics, the more outside observers are likely to view these actions as a product of the cult leader's personality and not at all owing to the cult setting. For this reason, lay writers have claimed that negative factors are identified as characteristic of religious leaders (Stoner and Parke, 1978). Actually, there are a number of psychological characteristics implied in the differentiation between traditional religious leadership and cult leadership, but, is there really a consistent pattern of negative personality factors that characterize cult leaders? Reviews of leadership literature clearly show a lack of consistent patterns of leadership traits for leaders over a wide variety of settings (Davis, 1969); Gibb, 1969).

Why have psychologists seemingly failed to find a strong relationship between personality factors and patterns of leadership? According to Gibbs (1969), a leadership expert, there is no evidence that there is a strong correlation between personality and leadership. He also suggests that the only thing we know for sure is that leaders, in general, tend to be more intelligent than their followers and they have higher self-confidence and self-esteem. Beyond this observation, leadership experts have noted that personality measures may not be very good predictors of behavior because situational factors are likely to impose constraints on leaders and their personality characteristics may be masked. In addition, the kinds of religious groups studied have been so different that consistent leadership patterns and personality characteristics have been difficult to isolate (Wilson, 1969). To say this is not to impugn the fact that some observers of present-day cult leaders believe that they are self-seeking Machiavellians who consciously manipulate their followers in an effort to gain wealth and power (Stoner and Parke, 1978). They are ready, like Nietzsche's "Super Man," to seek self-fulfillment by sacrificing their converts for their ideals. In spite of the fact that their homilies, on the surface, seem to have great merit, they often arouse great resentment in traditional religious leaders because they seem to believe that these cult leaders have an inability to compromise their utopian religious principles.

This is precisely where the difficulties lie, because cult leadership, like most charismatic forms of leadership, is too complex to show a strong relationship to personality factors without first taking into consideration the situation that gives rise to leadership in the first place. But this is where the bad news ends, because if we put aside the task of looking for personality characteristics of leaders, it is then possible to focus our attention on different cult leadership styles. If this is done, it soon becomes obvious that there is now evidence that in most situations more than one type of leader can emerge. For example, according to Robert Bales (1970), there are two very general styles of leadership: (a) *task leaders*, or those who seem to get the group's tasks done as efficiently as possible; and (b) *social emotional leaders*, or those who tend to create and sustain an acceptable psychological climate within the group. These are the leaders who are sensitive and responsible to the personal needs and problems of their group's members. According to Bales, all leaders use a combination of both of these leadership styles, some more than others.

Does Bales' theory have anything to do with an understanding of cult leadership? I would guess that it does because a cult leader's task and emotional style is important to the survival of the cult group. Then, if there are real differences in the leadership styles of cult messiahs and gurus, we need to know why they exist. Are they based on the pervasiveness of the cult setting or are they basic to all forms of absolute leadership?

People generally accept attitudes, values, and patterns of behavior of those around them, especially when they are committed to the goals of the group. If one is a member of a religious group, with an express desire to accomplish an urgently felt goal, like seeking a new life and personal salvation, absolute forms of leadership (autocratic leadership) may seem highly attractive. Paradoxically, then, if the stakes are high, a potential cult member may be more than likely to accept a charismatic leader. Perhaps, under these conditions the convert becomes more task oriented and emotionally dependent on a cult leader, especially in time of great need.

The most poignant factor that operates in favor of the cult leader is that potential converts have a need to respond to a strict code for behavior, despite their reputation for repudiation of the social system. It has been shown that most religious seekers have, prior to their cult conversion, already devoted themselves exclusively to a religious life (Singer, 1979). Then, the novice, upon entering a cult setting, usually is willing to give up all personal possessions and old ties for his new cult lifestyle and identity. Converts are expected to receive the cult leader passively and gratefully. They are not expected to take any role counter to their messiah's strict requirements for their cult conversion and membership.

But, along with faithful followers, the cult leader will attempt to convince potential converts that they can be saved through a special kind of cult salvation. For example, we know that when Moonie premies confess their sins for little external reasons, and learn that their confession is accepted by the Moon's leaders, this is taken as an expression of a need for cult redemption. The potential Moonies do not find themselves aloof from the cult group, and their feelings are not hidden from the cult's leaders. This is important, because as potential Moonies, it is appropriate for them to receive feedback from the group's participants. Hence, the group will help converts work through their needs for cult conversion. Faced with these strong social forces, converts express a wide range of emotions — including a "feeling of being born again" — if they experience these feelings (Sontag, 1977).

Because a cult like the Unification Church is negatively disposed toward the prevailing social system, a background of alienation and disillusionment is a significant common factor among potential converts. However, as I have already indicated, these are only necessary and not sufficient conditions to respond to the cult leader's appeal for conversion to the cult's ideology and religious dogma. The key factor here is the issue of how the person is strongly affected by the personal qualities of the cult messiah and the intense and compelling situational factors that dominate the cult setting (Sontag, 1977).

There are probably many factors that undermine the potential convert's unwillingness to resist the authority of a cult leader. Among the most apparent is the cult leader's style and manner of speaking. The cult leader, like Swami Prabhupada, may adopt a particular attire that is appropriate to the cult setting. The leader generally exhibits great expertise and commands great respect from those present. These trappings of the cult leader contribute to the recognized authority to lead. Most importantly, the leader fills both task requirements and the social emotional needs of converts perhaps because he or she possesses charisma and takes advantage of the cult situation. Hence, cult leaders derive their ability to influence followers from their special personal qualities to attract loyalty and strong commitment.

Understand that some cult leaders can influence people because followers are seeking a special kind of influence from a person they consider an attractive authority figure. For example, according to social psychologist Patricia Niles Middlebrook (1974), the females who joined Charles Manson's "cult family" did so because they sought a special sanctuary from the outside world and they sought those with similar antiestablishment beliefs and values. They also wished to achieve greater self-understanding, to establish a new or different lifestyle, and on a more pragmatic level, to enjoy group sex and drug experimentation. Most of all, these females were apparently attracted to the charismatic Manson; a messiah with a special message.

Although the charismatic Manson's "cult family" was not originally founded on religious principles, he managed to incorporate his special form of civil religion into his cult's "utopian plan." For example, during his incarceration, Manson read the Bible and selections from Hubbard's Scientology. This is when he decided that the *Book of Revelation* had predicted the coming of the Beatles. In effect Manson invented a religion that consisted of a strange mixture of the Beatles' lyrics (Revolution 9) and reincarnation. Later, he believed that the 1969 Tate-LaBianca murders would touch off a racial war and subsequently he would be established as the spiritual leader of the world (Bugliosi and Gentry, 1975).

In my discussion so far, I have not made it clear whether or not Charles Manson is a charismatic cult leader. In order to do this it is only relevant that we find that he had sufficient followers who endowed him with these special qualities. Then, a central element in Manson's charisma was his plan for religious salvation and his revolutionary pursuits. First it should be noted, however, that Manson's recruiting methods were not as obvious as those used by Moonies or Hare Krishna. For example, there were no street corner or airport solicitings, Manson attracted converts to his "family" by promising drugs and sex and freedom from the "establishment." Visitors to his California-based Spahn Ranch were asked to follow Manson only after they used hallucinatory drugs and engaged in group sex. He bound his devotees to him through drugs, religion, music, and the fear of punishment for disobedience. Male members of the "family" were allowed to come and go as they pleased. Manson's females, however, were forced to remain at Spahn Ranch under what has been described as "extreme forms of harassment."

Then, what "special power" made Manson attractive to his "family?" Followers, such as Sue Atkins, Linda Kasabian, and "Squeaky" Fromme all said that "his voice, his eyes, and his gentle persuasive manner" were important. These females claimed that Manson held them to him with a "hypnoticlike spell." He would sit for hours and strum his guitar, open his eyes wide, and stare at them. This is what made Manson's "girls" fall into a "trancelike state." Without doubt, Charles Manson is a charismatic cult leader. He euphemistically referred to himself as a *hymie*, a label he claimed meant a "religious leader." Manson's charismatic influence did not stop after his arrest and murder conviction; his "family" still remained faithful, keeping watch over his Death Valley "paradise."

Sadly enough, Charles Manson's "revolutionary cult" illustrates that when young followers take charismatics seriously, anything that tends to "keep their faith" places the leader in a favored position and contributes to the fanaticism of the cult. More to the point, cult leaders like Manson seem to have the qualities of Bales' social emotional leader and Weber's charismatic leader. Yet, as I have previously indicated, in situations where members are made to feel emotionally dependent on "revolutionary" cult leaders, members react when they or their leader are verbally abused by a public that disapproves of their leader or their political or religious ideals. These are the repercussions they suffer owing to having placed themselves against the "establishment." The more they feel inadequate and anxious, the more they look mainly to the strength of their leader, presumably his supposed "omnipotence" and "omniscience." Their strong emotional dependence on their leader retards their ability to challenge his absolute authority (Bugliosi and Gentry, 1975).

Perhaps the most important conclusion to draw here is that the individual who assumes the role of a cult leader may or may not fit the stereotype of an "unfettered sociopath," driven by "pathological needs" to destroy both himself and his cult followers. On the other hand, the claim that leaders like Jim Jones and Charles Manson are sacrosanct leaders who manipulate their followers and hold on to them through special techniques of "mind control" and "suggestibility" seems fairly well substantiated. Still, the special conditions of the cult setting, such as the emotional stress and alienation of the cult's members, and the amount of support and acceptance of the cult leader influences what the leader does. For example, it is well known that under conditions of stress and strong emotional need, cult leaders can become increasingly more authoritarian and radical than under nonstressful conditions (Lincoln and Mamiya, 1980).

The Handmaidens of Cult Leaders

In recent years large numbers of people have experienced a sweeping shift in their concerns and now seem to focus more than they did a generation ago on the societal institutions assumed to intrude on their personal freedoms. Some writers have observed that there is an increased trend toward self-absorption. Still others have suggested that there is a growing denial of individual responsibility for the social processes that guide and direct a democratic framework as the preferred means of attaining social and personal goals (Judah, 1978; Roof, 1978). Whatever the reasons are for this seemingly deflated reality, many people these days are having trouble believing in the American dream and in themselves. As I noted earlier, these are times when people are living in the midst of what seems to be day-to-day frustration, where the old promises of "work hard or study and you will achieve success" seems no less relevant. But, a new paradigm appears to be slow in emerging as a viable model for articulation on the societial level, or for social planning, that holds promise for both greater personal satisfaction and social survival, and, during this "age of trouble," cults promise what our social institutions have seemingly failed to deliver. We know that people who are drawn to religious cults seem to have deceived themselves into believing that happiness is a cult experience or an attractive alternative to feelings of loneliness and frustration. This is why for some people the cult is viewed by its members as a place where they can belong and realize their full potential.

Why are so many people dissatisfied with their lives these days? A few years ago, Robert K. Merton (1957) observed that a condition of *anomie* is a pervasive characteristic of some people in our society. This condition makes it difficult for some people to achieve individual or socially shared goals. That is, when conditions in society approach a state of normlessness for the individual, socially appropriate behavior becomes less clear and the unconventional behavior of "radical groups" can more easily become dislodged. This is so because at this time the person's values and norms become less anchored in mainstream society. This is especially likely to happen when people do not have access to legitimate means to reach their goals. Disjunction of goals, and means to achieve these goals, is experienced under conditions of *anomie*. The result is that barriers to full participation in society take place and, accordingly, people may ritualistically follow the routines of everyday life and attempt to affirm the values of society even when they seem to have given up on society's goals and values. Others may withdraw from society and seek comfort in drugs or alcohol or join a religious cult in order to pursue their goals.

I have emphasized the fact that young people who join cults are suffering from low self-esteem and that they seek a cult experience as one way to regain or increase their self-image. I have also indicated that cult converts have joined during periods of deep depression, confusion, and despair; when their lives seemed at the time meaningless (Singer, 1979). Nevertheless, Dorothy Corkhille Briggs (1970) reminds us that young cultists seek independence from their parents only to become highly dependent on their religious group. They adopt the religious beliefs of their cult rather than develop their own set of religious beliefs and values, and they do menial labor instead of developing occupational or professional goals. All this seems inconsistent because most cultists come from middle- and upper-class families where the traditional work ethic and educational goals are firmly entrenched (Singer, 1979).

According to Ernst G. Beir and Evans G. Valens (1975), when one atempts to understand cult people, one should consider how young religious seekers' attitudes and behavior are changed. This is done in a cult setting that disengages the person from the outside world and then provides the conditions necessary for the development of a cult lifestyle. This theme is familiar to social psychologists. For example, Daryl Bem's (1972) self-perception theory can be used to explain how people infer their attitudes and beliefs from observing their own behavior. In effect, people become an audience to their own behavior and then infer their attitudes from their behavior. People also infer others' attitudes and beliefs through observing what people do and say.

After appreciating Daryl Bem's theory, it does not seem unreasonable to conclude that a cult group establishes a supportive behavioral change framework for members to infer their cult-related beliefs. They do this by creating a setting for self-focus. For example, cult leaders and their total converts provide models for accepted cult beliefs and correspondingly appropriate behaviors. Moreover, every cult seems to have its share of cultists who claim they are saints or martyrs, and the most fervent believers are encouraged to model their behavior after them as they are urged to "keep the faith." All this takes place in spite of the convert's parents' opposition to their child's cult membership. As premies are exploited by their messiah or guru, they become more loyal to the group. There is even the suggestion that the more converts suffer a great deal to reach their objectives, the more firmly they commit themselves to their goal. It goes without saying that a close scrutiny of cults, like the Moonies or the Hare Krishna, reveal a chain of ever increasing commitment to the cult's practices.

To the extent that cult people are strongly influenced by their leader, it is proposed here that this influence creates for them a new and a different social reality. People who expend a great amount of effort to seek a different social reality will subsequently seek confirming evidence to support this reality. Consider the following example: If new devotees do not experience what the cult leader promises, they are asked to search within themselves for the answer or to wait until they grow more within the cult setting. Once converts are convinced, however, they can cling to the abstract and high purpose to which they espouse and resist any opposition to the cult membership from their former friends and family.

How far can the results of a cult membership extend? I have attempted to show that it can go beyond the limits of one's cult; it can modify the way the convert experiences social and physical reality. Under certain conditions, a cult membership can lead people to experience astonishing changes in their beliefs and, yes, in their personalities (Singer, 1979).

Prophets and Females: "Teaching Women to Know Their Place"

In preceding sections, I demonstrated how the cult movement is not very well anchored in our social system. I also indicated that cults share at least one common characteristic: they are only partially open to women because of their traditional view of females. One would think that, because cults claim to espouse an egalitarian ideology, they would encourage liberal attitudes toward females. According to Emily Culpepper (1978), on the verbal level, some religious leaders promulgate feminism; however in reality, the low valuation of women in cults is often expressed most directly in a common cult practice that demands that males be eagerly served as avatars by the cult's females. Most females are only tolerated as economic resources as they serve to advance the patriarchal lineage of the cult leader. Even in the cult's housework and child care, the female's tasks are under the direction of male cult members. (Stoner and Parke, 1978).

In short, little evidence exists to show that females, in any sizable proportion, encounter the attitude that they are equal to male premies. Hence, the question arises: "Why did a division of labor, based on sex, become the norm in the first place, given the ideology that cults purport verbally to support sexual equality?" One reason some women have left Reverend Moon's Unification Church or Swami Prabhupada's Hare Krishna movement is the great difference between an increasingly liberal American view and the more traditional Hindu and Korean view of women. This is especially true of the Unification Church, where cultural differences can be observed in the daily activities of "shared fellowship and love." To this point, young male and female premies are "love bombed," in their close living and working conditions; however, they are denied physical expression of sex, and females are blamed more than males for any violations of this seemingly strict Oriental code. We also know that in Hindu theology there are no holy women found in Indian temples. Hare Krishna consider feminism undesirable at best. For example, Swami Prabhupada claims that Krishna women are not interested in equality; "they're only interested in male love and acceptance" (Levine, 1974).

Given the seemingly precarious status of female cult members and an ideology that pushes females toward highly stereotyped and traditional sex roles, it can be concluded that cults enhance an atmosphere of female inferiority. Hence, the fate of females in cults suggests their special vulnerability; on the one hand they are asked to seek their destiny through following a male cult leader, and then as the drama unfolds they are asked to faithfully serve male converts. These certainly are challenges to one's beliefs in liberation. As a matter of fact, many feminists have already criticized the inferior status of women in such movements as the Hare Krishna, the Divine Light Mission, and the Unification Church (Culpepper, 1978).

So it seems that female cultists must, at least for the present time, assume the role of the "pampered menial" because they are not ceremoniously romanticized as are the male premies or the male charismatic leader. This is true even though there appear to be a few sectarian cults, less authoritarian than religious cults, in their organizational structure, for instance, Yogi Bhajan Kikhist's Healthy-Happy-Holy Organization (3HO). Yogi's 3HO claims a great number of ashrams nationwide and that "female premies live on an equal plane with their male counterparts." Nevertheless, in the 1980s, when many women are seeking more options for themselves, and are no longer denied as many equal opportunities as formerly, one can speculate that female cultists will want to explore these options, and as a result may leave cults in increasing numbers.

Some Final Comments on Cult Leaders and Their Converts

Earlier I pointed out difficulties in defining cult leadership. This is true because people often seem too inclined to think that cult leaders display behavior caused by their negative personality traits and they seem to neglect the strong situational factors that influence a cult leader's behavior. Indeed, some popular writers conclude that most cult leaders and their followers are psychologically disturbed or borderline psychotics (Stoner and Parke, 1979). Perhaps most of us have a particular "need" to see negative behavior as having its cause in bad character or personality traits (Miller et al., 1978). I will have more to say about this aspect of cult behavior later on.

The issue as to why people join cults becomes especially significant when we consider the social and personal factors of the cult leader that influence the person's cult conversion. Once an individual is converted to a cult membership, the cult group makes correct behaviors salient, and appropriate beliefs for its members become more binding. This is all made possible because many people are influenced without apparent conscious awareness of the source of this influence (Taylor and Fiske, 1978). This is why many former cult members claim that they never really knew how they became converted to their cult membership. In support of this observation, social psychologist Richard Nisbett and colleagues have demonstrated that people are not generally aware of their own cognitive processes. That is, not only do individuals not know what factors caused their behavior, they also misreport their cognitions. To this point, many cultists seem to reason that the cult leader told me what to do and how to think (Nisbett and Wilson, 1977). This is why, no doubt, countless thousands of unwitting young people have become "victims" of self-proclaimed messiahs or gurus without realizing what happened at the time.

The evidence presented so far clearly indicates that a cult lifestyle and identity constitute a highly salient basis for noncultists to differentiate the cultist from mainstream religion as well as the greater society. It is in this sense that people often view cult devotees as basically unstable, as lacking traditional values and beliefs, and as only marginal, if at all, contributors to society. Hence, by the mere fact of being different, cultists demonstrate their seeming lack of moral worth and their unrespectability, relative to the dominant cultural theme. The cult devotee is accorded a negative stigma and a special negative identity; this is the high cost of becoming a deviant religious seeker (Pavlos, 1979).

6

Are Cults Deviant
Religious Moorings?

Are Religious Cults Deviant?

According to the labeling perspective, the act of being labeled a cult leader or follower confers certain attributes on people. In this sense, a cult's leader and his followers are perceived as deviant by others and, in turn, the cult leader and his devotees may react to these labels by either accepting them or by denying them and counterlabeling their labelers (Matza, 1969).

When an individual or a group has been labeled deviant, other people usually make attributions about those labeled. For example, the deviant or stigmatized group may not be considered "normal" or "morally sound." Then, to say that a cult group is "crazy" or "mad" implies that the group ought to be treated as if the label correctly characterizes them. Cultists who have been labeled deviant are likely to be considered "fanatics" or even "politically dangerous" or "psychotics." Religious leaders, whose beliefs and practices challenge traditional religion, are likely to be relegated to low status because they oppose others' basic religious beliefs and values.

Yet sociologists report that people do not always agree on the relative nature of what is taken as deviant (Gibbons and Jones, 1975). This is true because in most cases people do not use consensus information when they judge the actions of others. To this point, people usually do not extensively utilize the opinions or beliefs of those who are not members of their own reference group when they construct their conception of what is taken as deviant behavior (Ross, 1977). This is not to deny that, for the most part, people in a particular culture tend to share a common view of their world and they take this view for granted.

Given this condition, it obviously becomes important to ask: "Under what circumstances are religious seekers labeled deviant?" When we ask this question we soon discover what is generally taken as nonnormative or deviant. For example, many present cults like the Unification Church or the Hare Krishna depart from what is understood as "normative religious practices and beliefs" according to those who espouse more conventional religion. For example, Reverend Moon makes his would-be messianic status obvious to his followers by refering to his wife as "the bride of Christ" and himself as the "Messiah" (Anthony and Robbins, 1976). These claims presumably have alienated Moon and his followers from traditional religious leaders. Some have labeled Moon "mad" or "crazy" (Stoner and Parke, 1978).

In this era of new religions it is of interest to note whether or not all cults can be considered deviant. From these kinds of considerations one can gain some insight into the workings of group-based deviancy (Pavlos, 1979).

Before discussing deviant religious behavior, it might be better to first note that a convert's cult-related behavior sometimes is interspersed with noncult activities. For example, some present-day cult members are involved in different aspects of their general community's traditional and institutionalized forms of social behavior. That is, a particular cult member may be highly committed to spending time in organized cult-related activity yet still continue to function as a full-time student, employee, parent, etc. It is here that the person's cult experience may not be all-embracing. For instance, most Scientologists continue to live, work, and play in the "outside world"; they attend school and work and are "contributing" members of society. This is necessary because they need cash to pay for the high price of tuition for Hubbard's Scientology programs, presumably needed to pursue their goals of "clear thinking" and "freedom of inner expression" (Marty, 1976). Given this situation, Scientologists have attempted to *normalize* their deviance through making accommodations. Perhaps, in such cases, people are more tolerant of deviations that only peripherally challenge traditional views. For example, people may react less negatively to those who practice only a part-time unconventional ritual, but tend to be less tolerant of those whom they perceive as fully imbued and committed.

Still, most cults, unlike Scientology, demand from their members a strange sort of full-time indulgence and great devotion to the cult leader and the group. These demands direct them away from the noncult world. I have previously referred to this phenomenon as *total environment* because cult members are required to develop a total cult-related lifestyle. This takes place when the cult develops a division of labor and followers are expected to live by the cult's rules, implied or expressed in its religious dogma. Norms for the curtailment of external relationships emerge. In short, social scientists would describe religious cults as groups that have both a normative structure and, often, a well-elaborated social organization. In Moon's Church there are explicit rules (norms) stating when and where the Moonies assemble and Moon demands that his followers practice his special religious ritual. Moon's practices are, no doubt, totally accepted by most of his members (Back, 1977). This is why cults like Moon's Unification Church can demand deviant religious practices and they can foster a seemingly "radical" ideology that tends to survive, in spite of opposition from traditional religion, even though there is a change in the cult's membership with the passage of time.

To this point, the religious rites and beliefs of cult leaders, such as Reverend Moon, tend to make extreme demands on their converts, especially followers who totally accept their leader as divine or as their special messiah. These young cult idealists seem to embrace the view that their leader has been chosen to do God's work. Their intense cult loyalty represents a great challenge to traditionalists. It is here that a cult group is likely to come under attack from the outside community and subsequently get labeled "crazy," "kooky," or "sick." Meanwhile, verbal attacks from the outside community are likely to increase followers' commitment to their religious leader. This provides them with a special kind of internal justification for their cult's existence. Moreover, once people label a cult's members as deviant, the convert's behavioral options are likely to become highly constrained. Therefore, people who label cult members, intentionally or unintentionally, can force these *stigmatized* converts to play out their assigned deviant roles (Lemert, 1972).

Being labeled deviant does not mean that those labeled accept the attributes imputed. Evidence suggests that people with a narrow *perceptual field* impute a deviant label to an individual or group on the basis of a particular attribute associated with a particular person or group (Guten, 1978). This is because one condition for the formation of a deviant identity is that perceivers observe only a small sample of a cultist's behavior. For example, the seemingly "strange" religious attire or ritual practiced by cults, such as the Hare Krishna, is often used by the media to label them "crazy" or "fanatics." This demonstrates that some people, who attribute negative characteristics to others, tend to use highly restricted *categories* or *coding systems*. They draw negative inferences from observing converts' unconventional behavior. Parents who object to their children's religion tend to use the deviant categories readily accessible to them because their attitudes toward the cult are salient, and they are negative in the first place (Fishbein and Ajzen, 1975; Stoner and Parke, 1978).

Indeed, to this point, there is evidence suggesting that groups labeled deviant (e.g., cults) do not always accept these group-based labels. That is, religious seekers may come to label their labelers "sinners." These negative counterlabels are more likely to be imputed when the outside community directs labels to the group rather than to the individual cult member (Gurwitz and Topol, 1978; Lerner, Miller, and Holmes, 1976). Consequently, cult converts often tend to view nonmembers, especially members of traditional churches and deprogrammers, as a "perverse and insidiously dangerous element" (Matza, 1969). A few cultists have claimed that members of their group have been falsely labeled psychotic. Some cultists have claimed that their cult friends have been placed in mental hospitals or have been kidnapped from their group (Edwards, 1978). This is why some cult members claim that these actions are an unlawful plot to destroy their cult. Cult followers who become irate are unlikely to accept the negative labels accorded them.

It now seems appropriate to define deviant behavior in order to develop the criteria needed to evaluate cults as forms of group-related deviancy. First, from a social psychological perspective, I understand deviant behavior to mean that when people observe a group (or an individual) that has persistently and voluntarily departed from socially accepted norms, they are likely to label the group deviant. Second, observers are likely to react negatively to the group and to attribute to the group negative characteristics. They then assume that these characteristics are the cause of the deviant behavior (Pavlos, 1979). The form that deviations take affects the degree of the negative reactions of others. For example, religious cults that use "deceptive techniques" to recruit members and to solicit money are more likely to become stigmatized than those who do not.

Consider the profound implications of this aspect of deviancy. When converts continue to deviate from the "acceptable" norms of the community, they may come to label their religiously oriented behavior as deviant. Social psychologists refer to this behavior as *self-attributed deviancy* (Pavlos, 1979). In line with this reasoning, it seems clear that there is ample evidence from theory and research showing that when people observe or hear about a young cultist, whose beliefs and behavior vary from their own, they are not dispassionate observers; they make attributions about what caused these beliefs and actions. At this point, if the young premie focuses on his or her own behavior, he or she too may come to infer that he or she is a deviant religious seeker. In other words, what attribution theorists claim is that the convert's self-labeled deviant beliefs can often follow from others' attributions and from the person's own self-observations (Bem, 1972; Guten, 1978; Pavlos, 1979). Thus deviancy may entail more than nonnormative behavior; it may consist of deviant beliefs and attributes. Finally, the individual may adopt a deviant identity (Guten, 1978).

The fundamental proposition of the labeling perspective is that powerful people, by making rules, create deviance; these rules are applied to those that are labeled deviant. However, consider still another explanation for deviant behavior. According to social psychologists John and Susan Darley (1976), research shows that individuals go through *choice points* before they are labeled deviant; for example: (a) Individuals must become aware that they are in strong disagreement with their parents or people in their community over an important belief. When this disagreement becomes more salient, they may decide to act against others and seek out social support from similar others. (b) This is likely to take place when they seem unable to bring their views in line with others and especially if they begin to treat them negatively. (c) When individuals seek out others, who share their beliefs and values, they then find social support for their previously challenged beliefs. (d) Since the individuals' new group is composed primarily of those who share a common deviant belief system, the group tends to become highly cohesive. Cohesive groups are especially likely to shape and control their members' behavior. (e) The group provides the social support necessary for its members to face great criticism and challenge from their former community and family. This is why people are highly likely to remain steadfast in their deviant beliefs and practices when confronted with opposing views from their former community.

Having conceptually linked the religious seeker's beliefs and actions to the concept deviance, I should now demonstrate more clearly when a cult can be considered a deviant religious group. As I have previously said, when a person assumes a cult lifestyle he or she begins to manifest behavior consistent with the cult group's expectations and comes to accept the view of his or her followers that outsiders are part of a hostile world. This is not the whole story because the convert may have intense feelings of disillusionment and alienation from the greater society or from his or her family, school, or work world.

What is labeled cult-related deviancy is primarily a matter of public behavior that departs from the established norms. This starts when the cult recruit discovers that in a cult setting there is constant attention and seemingly total acceptance for cult-appropriate behavior and beliefs. The rewards for this deviant behavior entail an absence of worldly distractions: no television sets, radios, or newspapers to remind one of the "hostile outside

world"; there is only "love bombing." New premies are never allowed to get lonely because they are never left alone to com-
miserate or to reflect on self-pity. From these conditions there
emerges a growing emotional bond that takes place during group
sharing sessions. All of this happens as confessionals are made by
premies about their former "worldly sins" and how they have been
born again or saved. Converts are strongly encouraged to read the
cult's sacred doctrine. As premies read, chant, pray, or meditate,
all of their worries seem to suddenly go away and a state of
euphoria comes naturally. Then, without expecting it, young
recruits experience a sudden change in beliefs. In order to shape the
premies' thinking, a special form of "mind control" is said to be applied by the cult's leader and this in turn produces what is labeled a
new altered state of consciousness (Stoner and Parke, 1978). This is
part of what gets labeled by popular writers and some traditional
ministers and priests as deviant behavior. When premies are labeled, and accept the labels, there may be no turning back. At this
time recruits are highly likely to become committed to a deviant
lifestyle because they have assumed the identity of the deviant
religious seeker.

Once the cult members are labeled deviant, this label is sustained
because converts tend to play out their role. This is one reason why
cultists appear to outsiders or to their family as "psychologically
disturbed." This illustrates that deviant labels are taken as global
statements about the entire personality and character of the convert.

The labeling perspective used by social scientists to characterize
deviancy is not without its problems. Walter R. Grove (1970) notes
that labeling theory cannot be applied to "mental illness" without
serious drawbacks. According to Grove, not all people who deviate
from the public's image of what is "normal" do so because of social
pressure; some suffer from "psychological disturbances." What do
popular writers and cult observers have to say about this? First,
they do not dispute the claim that most religious cults have a
deleterious affect on their followers (Conway and Siegelman, 1978;
Stoner and Parke, 1978). Recently, clinical psychologists have
studied ex-cultists (e.g., Singer, 1979; Swope, 1980) and have examined affidavits testifying that lasting psychological harm can

result from a person's *overcommitment* to a cult experience. Indeed, they claim that, in many cases, long-standing negative personality change can take place. For example, Margaret Thaler Singer (1979) reports that ex-cultists show a "blurring of mental capacity, an uncritical passivity" and other forms of what Singer notes are "signs of psychopathology."

So here we have a situation where we are caught between Scylla and Charybdis, attempting to figure out just what constitutes cult-related deviancy. But, there are several reasons for this problem. First, cult observers have not had a great quantity of psychological information available to them, relative to the characteristics of young converts. Second, most cult observers have not had the necessary training to adequately analyze the social and psychological aspects of cultists. Perhaps this is why the issue of religious cults had all but escaped psychological researchers until recent years. This strongly suggests that the basic assumptions about what is labeled deviant religiously oriented behavior may have been taken for granted or subsumed under the rubric of abnormal behavior or sociological theories of deviant behavior. Still, with the exception of a few studies (e.g., Festinger et al., 1956; Hardyck and Braden, 1962), there is a tendency to overlook the combination of social and personal factors involved. To this point, J. Stillman Judah (1978) suggests that we need research entailing random samples of cultists who have been deprogrammed and those who have dropped out of cults. They should be psychologically studied, using a blind evaluation where the psychologist does not know the status of the ex-cultists.

In the meantime, since cults exist in a social context that includes the cult as a reference group, it is important to consider the determinants of cultists' attitudes and religious beliefs and values since there still is a tendency to overlook the reasons that adolescents and youth turned to the new religions during the 1960s and 1970s. However, recently researchers have reached some tentative conclusions about why these young people joined or left religious cults. For example, one study suggests that defection from traditional religion and religious experimentation are associated with measures of alienation and dissatisfaction with the more traditional aspects of social life. The religious cult, then, is an alternative to those who are alienated from school, family, and their community (Wuthnow and Glock, 1973). These religious seekers differ from their counterparts who do not seek out the new religions. Wuthnow and Glock found that religious seekers, ironically, have higher grade point averages in high school and college (and are less concerned with grades). Religious seekers became involved in "radical" political groups, have experimented with drugs, and have more liberal views on sex. Nevertheless, religious seekers have many problems in relating with the opposite sex. Most importantly, these adolescents and youth report serious problems of identity formation, mate selection, and have great difficulty in stating life goals.

Cults, such as the Unification Church and the Hare Krishna, stress the breakdown of the American family and they offer converts what they say is the "perfect family." They give structure to the young person's life, especially those who accept their strict rules. Doress and Porter (1978) note that the cult makes clear distinctions between the benefits of communal living over more traditional nuclear family living. They stress the advantages of spiritual life over materialistic values, and austerity over extravagant living.

Although there is some research, well-developed theories to advance our understanding of cultists have been slow to emerge. Complicating this problem are issues relating to the unit of analysis or whether investigators should focus on the cult group per se or its individual members. There are several problems typically encountered in research on cults. In preceding sections I have suggested that many factors contribute to a cult lifestyle and the consequence of a cult identity may take many forms and directions. Nonetheless, scientific inquiry into cults should rest on the collection and analysis of data obtained in relatively controlled observational settings. To date, the numerous issues in religious cults have been rarely studied through the use of sound research methods. Without a direct assessment of the correspondence between actual behavior and reported behavior, one cannot be certain of how well reports of cultists agree with their actual practices and beliefs.

Since our society's notion of cult converts tends to create a common belief that they are psychologically disturbed, I should once again stress that there is little agreement on what causes young people to strongly commit themselves to a cult lifestyle. The few religious, sociological, and psychological scholars who have studied these problems all note that religious seekers are young idealists who have joined a religious group when seemingly more legitimate or traditional opportunities to develop a positive self-identity were perceived as relatively unavailable. These are the preconditions for a cult lifestyle but beyond these factors we have to look to the cult group for answers to the question whether or not cultists are deviant.

The cult condition alleviates the frustration and despair of occupational aspirations and frees members from family constraints and a desire to do well in school. Eventually a feeling of defenselessness and total acceptance on the part of the convert take place. Are these the necessary conditions that set the stage for labeling their beliefs and behavior deviant or for observers to denote that many cultists suffer from psychological disturbances? Perhaps so.For example, it is not too difficult to understand why cult observers like Carroll Stoner and Jo Anne Parke (1978) or Flo Conway and Jim Siegelman (1978) infer special negative motives behind religious seekers and their charismatic leaders. For instance, one conclusion reached by observers of cults is that these examples of deviant behavior are first encouraged by the cult leader and then reinforced by the cult group.

The power of a cult group to demand and get unconventional religious practices from its converts is illustrated by David "Moses" Berg's evangelism and his Children of God movement. In past years Berg and his nomadic children were found on street corners telling listeners that the comet Kohoutek would fizzle out and take Earth with it in an apocalypse never before witnessed in the history of mankind. Berg views himself as God's chosen messiah. In his MO letters (for Moses), he still tells his young devotees that sexual freedom is based on "true principles of Christianity." Disciples are told that they are given his special divine license to "sell their love and charms" to gain money to support the cause. Berg condones incest and claims that "God is very sexy because He often examines the nude bodies of young girls." According to Berg, his children confront God firsthand during sexual intercourse. In a MO letter from Berg he commented on how to avoid being arrested if confronted by the police. His special form of polygamy, practiced among his young female converts, has made his cult the object of legal action (Petersen, 1975; Streiker, 1977).

In addition to these more obvious forms of nonconventional religious practices and beliefs, a common characteristic of the Eastern religious cults, such as the Hare Krishna, is their require-ment that members take part in certain *intrinsically valued* stylized ritual, such as meditation, whereas little attention is paid to self-development or the premie's intellectual growth (Stoner and Parke, 1978).

Just why do many of the Eastern cults stress the significance of meditative ritual over personal growth? Is it because they wish to protect the premie's sense of self-worth from the exigencies of their noncult world or are they interested in protecting their way of life? Cult observers, who have asked cult devotees, say that converts ultimately seek to become one with God and for the present they are willing to practice the cult's ritual. They also claim that only with the help of their guru or Swami can they come to know God firsthand. Because these disciples are seeking what they label an "enlightened consciousness" they are relativizing their beliefs by "attuning these beliefs to a high state of being" (Levine, 1974).

Does all this suggest that these "self-validating experiences" are the bases from which outside observers label the cult deviant? And, most importantly, are these behaviors self-fulfilling because they make it increasingly more difficult for the observer to view these practices as "psychologically wholesome?" To this point, there is a "socially undesirable" aspect to the cult because it provides its followers with a *social visibility* replete with unconventional group-based deviant behavior. Central to this view, a cult provides its members with a special deviant identity that gets labeled by the outside community. This is why, no doubt, converts come to assume the role of the nontraditional zealot.

Then, deviant labels imply a relative continuity because they are constructed upon attributes assigned to the group and they appear to others to have stability and consistency over time. The caveat seem obvious: conformity to the cult's religious beliefs and prac-tices implies to the outside observer that the cult's religion is a special case of deviance because it is highly different from tradi-tional religion.

Dropping Out of a Cult

What generally happens when parents suddenly discover that a son or a daughter has been converted to what they consider a fanatic and deviant religious cult? Carroll Stoner and Jo Anne Parke (1978) claim that most parents seem to go through five stages of emotional torment (i.e., shock, confusion, anger, guilt, and a feeling of helplessness) as they become increasingly aware of the diminishing chances of regaining their child from the "gripping spell of the cult world."

Stoner and Parke relate many chilling and spellbinding personal chronicles of "cult madness" and they claim that very few cult members are able to leave a "bizarre and fanatic" religious cult by themselves. Yet, they note that many parents have decided to fight fire with fire, and in great desperation have employed deprogrammers to rescue their children. In their hope of recovering a son or a daughter some parents have even "kidnapped" their offspring from a cult. In this regard the former Moonie Christopher Edwards (1978) relates a detailed and dramatic account of how Moonies have resisted the "reverse brainwashing" techniques of their deprogrammers. He indicates that when deprogramming fails many converts drift back to an infantlike state of dependence on their cult.

Just what is deprogramming? It usually involves long hours of intense questioning and challenging of the cultist's beliefs before the young convert finally breaks down and begins to denounce his cult and its leader. As a matter of fact, deprogrammers, such as Ted Patrick and Tom Dulack (1976), claim that deprogramming is a necessary evil. This is why Patrick and Dulack indicate that deprogrammers attempt to discredit a cult leader in the eyes of the young cultist and they try to make the conflict more salient between the cultist's religious beliefs and what the deprogrammer considers a more rational lifestyle. While all this is going on the deprogrammer looks for a "breaking point." When this comes, the cultist is encouraged to denounce his cult leader and his religious beliefs and practices. For example, psychologist Daniel Batson tells about a "successfully deprogrammed Moonie" who said: "they showed me how the Church had twisted the Bible around. I finally opened my mind and admitted I was wrong. That was the hardest thing to face." On the other hand, Batson describes a situation where an "unsuccessfully deprogrammed Moonie" recounted a very different story about his experience with deprogrammers. The Moonie said: "you are forced to sit and listen and repeat what they say. They'll keep you there for however long it takes. It's so obvious to me who's wrong" (1976, p. 181).

In spite of these kinds of reports, many young people have claimed that they have been rescued from a cult. Some even claim that they have been returned to a more "normal life" as a contributing member of their community. This suggests that there are pros and cons regarding deprogramming and this is why the issue has often been taken before the courts.

Many cult members fear and despise deprogrammers more than they do any other single group. Some have even escaped from deprogrammers only to return to their cult in a state of what deprogrammers label "floating," or a condition of almost complete indecision where the cultist cannot adequately face the conflict between his cult life and the seemingly hostile outside world. It seems clear that all too often the highly structured life of the cult wins out and the cultist becomes even more committed to an "extreme cult lifestyle" (Slade, 1979).

What happens when a cult member is a minor? In such cases a few state courts have ruled that parents can indeed prevent their young offspring from joining a cult. However, the story is different when an adult-age son or daughter joins a cult. In this case parents may, if they desire, seek appointment as conservators, but only when the cultist is judged to be so "psychologically disabled" that he or she cannot manage his or her own property or money. Nevertheless, in most cases parents are appointed by a court official as conservators generally on a very temporary basis. When the appointment is more permanent parents can, if they choose, authorize a deprogrammer or the local police to remove their offspring from the cult scene. It all stops here, however, because as conservators, parents are not authorized by the courts to employ a psychotherapist to help their child nor can they easily commit their offspring to a mental hospital. Finally, some judges have decided that deprogramming is in point of fact illegal. What is more alarming, most deprogrammers are not trained to deal with the "psychological problems" of the young religious seeker. Even most psychiatrists and psychologists are not really trained to deal with the special problems faced by cultists.

Meanwhile, some converts have even taken their parents to court and sought their constitutional right to join a cult regardless of how unacceptable the cult's religion or ideology is to their parents. This claim is, of course, based on the U.S. Supreme Court ruling that holds that courts cannot and should not question the validity of a person's religious beliefs. At this writing there is litigation pending testing whether or not parents and their deprogrammers are not themselves in violation of federal civil rights laws when they attempt to stop a cult from influencing their children (Slade, 1979; Stoner and Parke, 1978).

So it would seem that most popular writers claim that cults do indeed have a deleterious effect on the lives of converts. Nevertheless, there is little hard or direct evidence testing this claim, using appropriate research methods; all there is are countless affidavits testifying to the "poor mental health" and confusion of cult members, especially those who are about ready to be deprogrammed (Singer, 1979). On the other hand, even though cults have been accused of using coercion and "brainwashing techniques" on their members, countercharges can be made when we consider the techniques used by deprogrammers to change unwitting cultists. When a deprogrammer claims that he or she has "successfully deprogrammed" a convert, he or she all too often leaves the ex-cultist in what appears to be a "state of limbo." For example, a young Moonie who claimed that he had been deprogrammed told me that he had neither returned home nor to his parents' religious faith, but instead was seeking still another charismatic cult leader, "this time a cult more rewarding and more spiritually meaningful than the *Divine Principle* of Reverend Moon."

What about those who have dropped out of a cult on their own accord? Have the critical newspaper articles and the negative versions of cult life presented on television talk shows had an influence on converts' decisions to leave their cult? Has there been a kind of "self-deprogramming" process for those led away from the "promised land" or the seeming martyrdom of a cult lifestyle? Before an answer to these questions can be given it should be understood that different forces operate when a cultist leaves a cult on his own in contrast to cases where a cultist is "taken from the arms of his cult leader." It would also be helpful if we knew more about why some women leave a cult on their own, like the Hare Krishna or the Unification Church. Is it because of the seemingly great contrast between the contemporary American view of feminism and the more traditional Hindu or Korean position of complete male dominance. Could it be that there is something new stirring in the depths of the female's religious consciousness? Does this mean that females may eventually demand equality and fair treatment from their male counterparts? For the moment there seems to be little evidence of equality and it appears that both male and female cultists have failed to perceive feminism as an important factor worthy of their attention. This is why, no doubt, the "cult movement" may some day be in serious trouble because the trend to trivialize or ignore these issues is likely to produce even greater dissatisfaction than there now is among female members. I think this is true because females are highly likely to feel an ever increasing sense of alienation from full and equal participation in cults and eventually they may come to do something about this in ever increasing numbers (Culpepper, 1978).

The "Aches and Pains" of Postcult Adjustment

Since there is a great difference between a religious cult experience, which stresses communal living and total acceptance of cult members, and traditional religion, it has been observed that many former cultists generally face difficult problems as they go about attempting to readjust to a postcult lifestyle (Cohen, 1975). The cult gave them a certain sense of pride and for some it created a feeling of elitism; after they leave their cult, no doubt, some are confronted with feelings of shame and guilt. No longer do they have the strict discipline, which was so important to them, to fall back on. Many drawbacks that were not obvious in the cult are now salient. Obedience to an authoritarian cult system seemed to prevent these feelings from emerging, and personal ambition and competitiveness, which are an integral part of the greater society, is missing in the cult. The personal and social forces that drove the person to a cult in the first place, the search for a special identity and the avoidance of alienation and disillusionment with the American dream—a pervasive theme in the devotee's precult experience—has now been transformed to a feeling that there is a struggle for survival in an unfriendly and seemingly hostile society. The great challenge for the ex-cultist is that he or she must overcome what has been described as great feelings of dependence. These feelings are still embedded in the individual's former cult experience. Leaving a cult means taking time out to be without former friends. It is a time to explore one's own feelings for one's self, to implode an energy usually directed outward. It is here that the young ex-cultist may come to feel that former cult peers cannot become free as long as they are humiliated and oppressed. This may produce feelings of guilt, especially when the ex-cultist ignore's the strivings of his or her former peers. Hence, the question that often arises when a cultist leaves the cult is "How does one who has been taught that the outside world is worthless and something to be despised come to accept this very same world as a compelling aspect of his or her postcult life?" So it seems that a great challenge for the ex-cultist is to develop a noncult identity and overcome the scars of a cult lifestyle so deeply embedded in his or her former cult identity. This seems true because the person's cult experience epitomized the development of cynicism and resignation. However, always underlying this cult theme is the feeling of childlike dependency and indecision. The dream is gone, the cult experience promised to be, for many, an alternative way of life where inner happiness could be developed through sacrifice and hard work for God. When the cult world is left behind there is a kind of cold hard reality to face and the young cultist has been ill-prepared to meet this challenge.

The journey out of the cult has led a few former cultists to reaffirm their new status by taking the role of the countercult activist. They work with deprogrammers to liberate cultists from what they label an "exploitative and oppressive environment." Movingly, they tell of their concern for those who are still victims of the cult world; however, they are for the most part ill-prepared to do their craft. As a matter of fact, it now appears that many of these countercult activists are extremely antagonistic; they are vigorously vindicating their negative cult experience. This is why Stoner and Parke (1978) claim that today's most fanatical Moonie is often tomorrow's most dedicated countercult activist.

Margaret Thaler Singer (1979) has done clinical research and has seemingly identified emotional problems likely to be faced by ex-cult members as they attempt to reenter mainstream society. For example, she claims that it takes from six to eighteen months for readjustment to a postcult life to take place. In the meantime most of the hundred or so ex-cultists she worked closely with expressed feelings of depression and regret for having wasted an important part of their formative years in a cult. They also expressed feelings of loneliness and indecisiveness. They often slip into altered states of consciousness and episodes of "floating," not fully realizing whether or not they still are with their former cult associates. There is always the fear that cult members will somehow find them and punish them or that they will be damned by their cult leader. Singer claims that ex-cultists are generally obsessed with the question of why they joined a cult in the first place. Often there are feelings of guilt and shame that emerge as the ex-member attempts to justify former "deceptive fund raising and recruitment techniques." Many ex-cultists have serious sex problems owing to the strict sexual prohibitions they were taught in their former cult group.

The Future of Cults?

Since many current disciples of the "cult movement" have turned to the new religions in order to fill a void found in their traditional childhood religious experience, it seems necessary to systematically examine what has gone wrong. Why have so many of these people left the church of their parents? Although religious experts do not seem to have a precise answer to this question, they claim that traditional churches must do some serious "soul searching" (Kelley, 1972). Perhaps the answer lies more with the apparent general void young religious seekers have found in our traditional social institutions, including the family, our educational system, and our ever increasing big government. Meanwhile it seems that these young "people of prosperity" are, in greater numbers today, plagued by transient feelings of dissatisfaction and continuing to explore new directions out of this impasse by becoming ever more likely to seek out a new religious experience. The reader must be asking: "Are these young people choosing the best of all possible alternatives?" We need to seek answers to this question because the wide ripple set in motion by the current cult movement has had its share of "casualties."

Will the future demonstrate that the new religions will become more flexible and will they show a greater sense of responsibility for what is considered a "more healthy interest in the problems of society" instead of focusing on self-indulgence and "mind-controlling techniques," or will some of today's cults continue to exploit young idealists? Will there be more of what the new religions say they represent rather than the dogmatic practice they in reality support? At present this is dramatically illustrated by their lack of involvement in society's affairs. We need to know whether or not cults will continue their preoccupation with "divine fate control," or will they come in time to espouse more moderate religious and political themes? Can the cult movement shrink back to the more common goals of traditional religion? Can these religious seekers strive for self-sufficiency and still win their battle over feelings of powerlessness? Will the future of these new religions see them concentrate on making their devotees happy while at the same time encourage them to pursue traditional educational and career goals? In spite of some expressed optimism, chances are that cults will change little, if any, unless the social conditions that give rise to them in the first place are ameliorated.

For the moment it does appear that many cults have peaked. But this is where the good news ends: The dissatisfaction with traditional religion is still present. Meanwhile, on a more pragmatic level, readers may want to know just how to recognize a potential religious seeker when they meet one. Young cultists are likely to cut off lines of communication with their parents or friends, use "stereotyped language," and speak of being saved through an apparently "strange religious conversion" (Stoner and Parke, 1978). In addition, many young devotees attempt to deceive their parents by telling them that they have joined a religious group that is concerned with world peace and spiritual tranquility. These days, however, parents are likely to become suspicious, especially when a son or daughter has given up on a college education in order to pursue these newly found religious goals (Stoner and Parke, 1978). If parents know how to interpret these "behavioral signs" they can in time, if they oppose their child's religious choice, stop the cult from forging its influence. In addition to looking for these "behavioral signs," parents can look for changing values and beliefs that seem linked to a new religious orientation. Most importantly, when the young person accepts a cult's ideology this may reduce the likelihood of a "rational form of dialogue." For example, a young religious seeker may claim that God predicts a millennium overthrow of evil that is inevitable in the next few years. The person may claim that he or she is working for worldwide salvation. Some cult children may make it clear that they are seeking a new identity, trying to escape loneliness, or eager to experience a new sense of spiritual meaningfulness. They may even attempt to communicate these beliefs to their parents in the hope of receiving their approval (Cohen, 1975; Rice, 1976).

Parents should realize that when their son or daughter claims he or she is seeking help from the supernatural, and that he or she is rejecting orthodox religion in search of spiritual salvation and a new identity, he or she may hint of a religion or an ideology that prophesies the destruction of contemporary society (doomsday cult). The young convert may suggest that this "supernatural transformation" will be accomplished by a messiah or guru who claims the power to create a new world of bliss and everlasting peace (Stoner and Parke, 1978). These are some of the reasons why parents should attempt to determine if a son or a daughter is in a cult. They should seek answers to questions like the following: (a) What are the religious organization's goals and values? (b) Does the group attempt to radically change a member's personality? (c) Is it aimed at changing society with the central idea of focusing on or gaining great financial strength? (d) Do they isolate members and preach that society is evil and that its devotees should help put a stop to evil and sin by turning to a charismatic religious leader? (e) Does the movement claim that it is a vehicle through which already existing alienation can be expressed or remedied?

If parents disapprove of their child's religious choice they can look for certain "signs or key factors" that seem to suggest that their child is motivated to gain commitment and conversion to one of the new religions. Parents can do the following:

1. Look for a strong conflict between their child's early religion and the existence of a religion that calls for great personal sacrifice.

2. Ascertain whether or not there is a willingness on the part of their child to abandon more "rational principles" or to defend a particular view or to defend an absolute religious truth.

3. Check to see if their child has developed an "aberrant interpretation of accepted eschatological principles."

4. Ascertain whether or not there is an intolerance of opposing ideologies and whether or not their child supports "metaphysical polarities" or "religious absolutisms."

5. Take stock of the fact that some good postdictive evidence shows that a few young cultists at one time or another have suffered from severe depression and that some have been described as "borderline psychotics" (Beir and Valens, 1975).

Nevertheless, this is not to imply, or even strongly suggest, that most cult devotees are psychologically disturbed. The reader should realize that, in general, young cultists seem to have great trouble believing in themselves; for the most part they are disillusioned idealists struggling to come of age during a time that makes it difficult to find a positive identity. This is what makes them especially vulnerable to a charismatic cult leader's attempt to establish a cult identity for them.

In the present chapter I have traced what happens when people develop a certain "cult mentality" and assert their identity in the full pride of their cult religious experience. I have attempted to show that under these conditions things are bound to go wrong, especially when cultists oppose or challenge traditional religion or secular interests. From these observations, it does not seem rash to conclude that the modern cult movement will face problems of unsettlement especially in a time when national and world conditions seem to challenge most organizations for survival. Then, from this perspective, on the face of it, it appears paradoxical that most major cults have grown and others have peaked whereas traditional religion has experienced some rather serious setbacks. This is true in spite of the fact that most religious cults have not yet developed the apparatus to sustain themselves in history, whereas traditional religion has already proven itself. Having said this, I will next attempt to assess the current status and destiny of cults.

7

The Current Status and Future of Cults

Myths and the New Religion

Because of the ever presence of the new religions, it is likely that certain misconceptions about them and their leaders will be perpetrated indefinitely. The present setion is devoted to examining these misconceptions, so that those who are interested in religious cults may be able to detect these misconceptions when they are encountered. This seems necessary because the workings of a cult are often notoriously elusive. Addressing this point, Harvard's Divinity Professor Harvey Cox (1978) admonishes those who criticize present-day cults from the vantage point that they often fail to take into account what he labels the *deep structures* of the cult's religious dogma. Why do people fail to take into consideration the official religious dogma of a cult (its deep structures), especially when they attempt to assess a cult's membership and its leader? Do traditionalists deliberately misrepresent religious cults because they have a great deal of difficulty projecting themselves into the cult situation? To this point, there is little doubt that many writers describe religious cults entirely from the point of view of former cult devotees or deprogrammers, who are often "victims" of a cult and their special biases intrude. In order to support this claim, Professor Cox outlines four *themes* or *myths* about the new religions he says are widely promulgated among writers.

Subversion is involved when critics assume, without solid evidence, that all civil religions (those with political influence) pose a great threat to a society's civil order. For example, Cox suggests that some "Moon watchers" have claimed that Reverend Moon's Unification Church is really a right-wing political front for a Korean anti-Communist movement, formally headed up by no less than South Korea's Chung Hee Park. According to this view, Moon's evangelism here in America is designed both to recruit great numbers of followers and to use these people to influence American legislative action in favor of Moon's activities in South Korea. While all this is going on, young Moonies are said to be unwitting dupes in an international conspiracy to protect South Korea from communist threat. The "evidence" used to support this claim comes from "Moon watchers" who have observed that before his death, Chung Hee Park did support Reverend Moon's Unification Church. To this point, it is necessary to stand back and evaluate what is really known about Reverend Moon's assumed political influence in Korea. When this is done it is important to question whether or not Moon has enjoyed a special kind of diplomatic immunity in South Korea. Consequently, it would appear that there may be several possible reasons why the profundity of these charges can be questioned. Indeed, Professor Cox notes that the main problem with cults such as the Moonies is not that critics always disagree with what a cult teaches, but that they often claim that cults have the potential for subversive action. Needless to say, the motives behind Sun Myung Moon's religious movement in Korea (as well as in the United States) are less than clear, leading to speculation about the purpose of Moon's elaborate organization. Nevertheless, the reason why Reverend Moon has been accorded high status in South Korea, no doubt, is because of his widespread lucrative in-dustrial interests there. This does not allow us to conclude, however, that Moon's theocratic teachings are a cover-up for subversive political aspirations. The best information about the movement is that it is often vivid and attention-getting; direct evidence to support the claim that Moon has great potential to subvert Korean or American leaders remains to be substantiated, however. Meanwhile, Moon's church is attempting to increase its membership and its industrial interests in Seoul are still prospering (Stoner and Parke, 1978).

The *myth of accusation* deals with what Cox claims are unfair attacks on the character and integrity of religious leaders. For instance, some "Moon watchers" have accused Moon of possessing "extraordinary and deviant Oriental sexual prowess." Critics have also claimed that Moon's movement is made up of countless sexual deviants and drug addicts (Stoner and Parke, 1978). To this point, I submit that psychologists and psychiatrists who have worked with ex-Moonies dispute these claims. In considering the implications of these accusations, it becomes incumbent on cult observers to document their claim that sexual deviants and drug addicts have gained membership in the Unification Church in great numbers. Quite aside from these general accusations, the evidence for deleterious effects, stemming from membership in the Moonies, is gleamed largely from affidavits testifying to the precarious mental health of Moonies. Perhaps the most important conclusion is that members of Reverend Moon's Church have been subjected to "mind control techniques." Although not conclusive, some empirical evidence tends to support this claim (Singer, 1979). This certainly does not demonstrate that Moon's followers are deviants in the sense that they have been accused.

Dissimulation, as illustrated by Cox, entails the myth that communication with religious cult members is all but impossible, or at best misleading, because cultists have been taught to deceive and lie. To this point, it is well known that Moon's "children" do in fact use "heavenly deception" on unwitting contributors to the Church or to recruit members for Moon. Notwithstanding, in spite of these charges, it is well known that once a person becomes an ardent religious seeker, he or she usually clings to his religious ideology and practice. Hence, no less than those deeply committed to a more traditional religion, cult members often attempt to justify their calling even if this does entail deception and persuasive techniques. Why do many traditional religious writers and cult observers conclude that converts lie and deceive their parents? Perhaps this conclusion derives from the observation that cultists have been reported to have a lamentable tendency to lapse into jargon, to use what appears to be neologisms in order to promote their cult religion. This is especially true when converts adopt the behavior required of their cult leader's ritual. Nonetheless, whether or not most cultists are taught to deliberately lie, other than to promote their cult's religion, is open to question.

The *Myth of the Evil Eye* is said to operate when conventional writers suggest that no sane person could truly ever don cult robes to take up a cult ideology. Writers often assume that cults always entail strong negative factors because they attract only those who are, at best, borderline psychotics. Some cult observers have even assumed that cult members must have been involuntarily taken into a cult through some diabolic force, witchcraft, or some mysterious brand of hypnotism. For this reason one can easily understand why those who make these charges do not recognize or appreciate the subtle but powerful social forces that exist in a cult group setting. Most people, like you and me, however, would find it difficult to resist explaining a cult's membership in psychopathological terms. Yet, as I have shown, another view of cultists can be advocated. For instance, the process of conversion to a cult ideology entails an awareness of one's unconventional religious beliefs. These are brought in line with the external events found in the cult's setting. Nevertheless, modification of a convert's views of the world takes time, but this is aided by the repeated encounters with those who advocate a view of the world partially consistent with the young convert's religious beliefs. From what is known from the limited data available on young religious seekers, it appears that they are disillusioned and frustrated people attempting to cope with a serious identity crises. This does not imply that all or even most cultists are psychologically disturbed.

Cox's urgent tone suggests that many myths exist about cults that have their origin in a cult observer's special biases. To this point, Cox implies that the reason why many writers are interested in exotic cults in the first place is that religion is the cry of the oppressed that something is wrong. Taken in this sense, it appears that when cultists are asked to make a great sacrifice for their group, their actions have been labeled psychotic by a few mainstream religious scholars as well as members of the mass media. So it would seem that old habits die hard because it seems vitally important that they support popular stereotypes of cultists (Cox, 1978).

According to Professor Cox, many present-day evaluations of cults are based not only on illogical considerations but also on special biases and popular stereotypical thinking. A careful analysis of recent newspaper and television accounts of the cult movement reveal some of the myths Cox warns against. Hence, the strong biases that operate in newspaper and television descriptions of cults is especially obvious as writers tell stories of "bizarre cult leaders." For example, mass media accounts of cult-related behavior place the blame for cults on what they label the "strange and pathological personalities of cult leaders" (such as Reverend Moon), whereas still other popular accounts place the entire blame and responsibility for cults on what is labeled a "sick society" (Krause and Stern, 1978).

How can we account for this strange twist of logic? Evidence exists that when outside observers (e.g., members of the mass media) view what they label deviant behavior they all too often tend to give too much weight to what they believe are people's personality characteristics or attitudes as the cause of deviant behavior (West et al., 1975). On the other hand, those who are labeled deviant are more likely to assume that the cause of their own behavior stems from the powerful situational factors they confront (Nisbett and Wilson, 1977). For example, cultists blame society for their reaction against society. Converts tend to view society as pervasively evil and corrupt and they react to society on the basis of these attributions.

I strongly suggest that if writers are to understand a cult's unconventional practices, they need to take stock of the events leading up to a cult conversion. Writers need to understand the strong personality characteristics and the unconventional religious beliefs of converts. They should consider the converts' intentions in choosing to pursue a particular religious course of action. Cult observers would do well to remember that both personal and social factors are at work. This is important because in a complex society like ours not all people can be provided with the kind of satisfactions they desire. Much of what goes on in cults can be attributed to the fact that many young religious seekers feel very uncertain about their future these days and they are doing something about their disillusionment and despair by joining cults or politically oriented groups. On balance, there is little question that the social conditions that create widespread dissatisfaction also foster the development of politically oriented protest groups and the new religious groups. People who are attracted to these groups often enjoy only marginal acceptance by the greater society. Evidence to support this view is provided by researchers like Daniel Yankelovich (1974).

The Current Status of Cults

How to evaluate the current status of religious cults is not a simple process. I have traced the evolution of several new religions, each of which has aided in my understanding of them. These groups are constantly changing, however, because they often confront new situations and opposition to their beliefs. At this point, I must stand back and evaluate some of these changes that are still in progress. I also have to go one step further and predict what I believe is the future of religious cults in America. Complicating this task is the lack of firsthand information and accounts.

What about the current status and future of cults? First, I propose that with the passage of time and the change of events some of the survival characteristics of many present-day cults will abate. Second, there are signs that the "cult movement" is on a plateau, engaged in holding on to a membership that may be weakening. For example, religious cults such as David "Moses" Berg's Children of God are less effective these days in recruiting new followers. What has happened to Berg's Children of God?

David Berg started his religious career as a Missionary Alliance Minister, pastoring a church in Arizona. After a short tenure in Arizona, Berg became the director of a coffee house in Huntington Beach, California, calling his ministry Teens for Christ. At this time, Berg taught Bible study and established a communal pattern of living. Followers were encouraged to quit their jobs or drop out of school and devote full time to the group. A turning point in Berg's movement took place in 1969 when he claimed that he had received a prophetic message, telling of the end of the state of California by a great earthquake. Berg, just as the biblical Moses, gathered his followers and set out to win converts, warning them of the catastrophe to come. Converts walked the streets and beaches in sackcloth and ashes, exhorting "sinners" to "come to Jesus before it is too late."

Late in 1969, a "crisis" occured when David Berg's wife caught him sleeping with his secretary, Maria. In order to absolve his "sins," Berg claimed that he had received a prophecy telling about the "Old Church" and the "New Church." He declared that Maria was the "New Church" and that Jane, his wife, was the "Old Church." Berg told his faithful devotees that God gave him Maria and took Jane.

The major religious and ideological goals of COG have undergone many changes over the past twelve years. From 1968 to 1969, most of the COG were born-again Christians. Then, late in 1969 things took a turn for the worse when Berg wrote his first MO (for Moses) letter and revealed a "new ideology" to his young converts. This is when he encouraged his youthful followers to engage in what he labeled "free sex," to drink alcohol, and turn to homosexuality and lesbianism. He promoted topless bathing and demanded that his girls do not wear panties. This is also when he introduced what he called a "Flirty Fish Ministry" in which he encouraged "fornication for the purpose of winning converts." Children conceived through Flirty Fishing were called Jesus Babies. Berg's MO letters also turned his children onto pornography, spiritualism, and astrology. Then, in 1978, after many young followers were scripted to David Berg's COG, he renamed them the Family of Love.

Trouble began when the California State Attorney General's Office started to look into Berg's religious organization. For David Berg, the struggle came down to his identity as the leader of his Family of Love versus the very existence of his movement. The fate of Berg's organization rested with his vulnerability as a "God-inspired despot." In order to resolve this problem, he claimed to have received what he labeled another prophecy, telling him to take the organization's money with him to Europe. This was made possible since the money raised by the Children went directly to David Berg and his son Jonathan (Bishop Hosea).

At this writing, David "Moses" Berg still writes MO letters and orders his faithful followers to form small groups for "security purposes." Berg's "new strategy" calls for door-to-door witnessing, peddling his cult's MO letters, organizing home Bible studies, and selling Berg's Worldwide Mail Ministry (Hopkins, 1978).

Since David Berg is the key person in this drama of cult leadership, what is the future of COG (Family of Love)? At the heart of Berg's problem, like many "far out cult leaders," is that once his movement blossomed his design for utopia became interspersed by periods of "paranoia" and a struggle with legal authorities, weakening its organizational integrity. This is why the future does not look promising. More and more young people are defecting as they become turned off, disenchanted with Berg's inner circle of faithful converts (Hopkins, 1980).

In the meantime, as already noted, Jimmie T. Roberts' "Garbage Eaters" is yet another example of a "far out" nomadic religious cult experiencing great trouble recruiting new converts.

Roberts, the ex-Marine from Paducah, Kentucky, calls himself Brother Evangelist. His youthful followers dress in long robes, follow the Brother around from city to city, eat out of garbage cans, and practice "free sex." Why all this "sacrifice" for Roberts? He claims that his children are God's chosen people. The Brother tells his converts "no marriage license, no minister, no vows." He teaches them to speak what is reported to be a "foul tongue" as these "dirty nomads" practice Roberts strict cult religion. Female members are taught by the Brother to obey their cult husbands and that "child abuse is God's way of ensuring obedience." Roberts urges his female followers to beat their children, claiming that this is necessary for their salvation (Sneed, 1979).

Jimmie T. Roberts' movement took shape about eleven years ago when he preached that God saved many people from the Great Flood and He would also save the Brother's converts. This is when Roberts sought recruits from college campuses. Over the years the movement has not proven very "successful." If anything, he has lost most of his members because they have found that the Brother's requirement that they follow him, crisscrossing the country looking through restaurant trash cans for food, is more than they bargained for (Sneed, 1979).

The obvious difficulties and problems faced by religious cults such as the Children of God or the "Garbage Eaters" is not to be found in Transcendental Meditation. This is true because Maharishi Mahesh Yogi's converts have "kept up with the changing times" and have produced several major modifications in the movements' religion and practice over the past twenty years. For example, in 1959, when Hindu Yogi's religious movement was incorporated, as a nonprofit religious organization (the Spiritual Regeneration Foundation), its stated purpose was to "encourage and develop spiritual growth, world peace, and happiness, through a system of deep meditation." However, when a number of noted celebrities saw fit to leave TM, so did the Yogi's Hindu religion. That is, in order to save his movement from extinction, the Yogi dumped his religious jargon in favor of a more scientific and psychological focus, claiming that meditation teaches people to live in a complex society. Because of Yogi's business acumen and leadership, the movement is "alive and well" today and claims a large following of devotees in the United States. They reportedly have over 6,000 teachers and an annual income of well over $20 million.

Obviously, the generalization to be induced here is that interest in TM will continue as long as its members gain personal satisfaction through meditation. At this writing, many of TM's devotees have still held on to their traditional American religious beliefs and meditate according to the sacred Hindu format. In time the Yogi may even give up his attempt to teach his most faithful adherents how to levitate and fly (Petersen, 1975).

If Maharishi Mahesh Yogi's TM seems to be doing well, the same cannot be said of the Divine Light Mission. Even though Guru Maharaj Ji is still very much the recognized leader of the Mission in the United States, his status in India is less secure. For instance, the Guru's mother and brother, who are in charge of the Mission in India, have little or nothing to do with the "untouchable little pudgy Indian holy person." This happened when the teenage Guru's lifestyle took a materialistic turn. He developed a passion for drinking, rock-and-roll dancing, Rolls Royce cars, and a formerly forbidden food—meat.

In 1972, the Maharaj Ji, who by this time had a passion for beautiful girls, married his "voluptuously beautiful" twenty-five-year-old American secretary. Of course, the Guru's liberated lifestyle did not set well with his family, and they sought to replace him. Ji managed to come through the controversy retaining his title and a few faithful followers, however. If the Guru should go public and confess and repent for his sins, in this time of compassion for sinners, his Mission may get back on course (Stoner and Parke, 1978).

In recent years, this is not all that's gone wrong with the Divine Light Mission. The Guru has faced many serious financial problems. For example, Maharaj Ji's Houston Astrodome millennium celebration left the Mission with debts that have been difficult to repay, even though the movement is still working hard to get back on a sounder financial basis. It all happened when the Divine Light Mission announced that a most significant historical event was to take place. Ji and about 20,000 faithful followers convened at Houston's Astrodome (80,000 were expected). Parking spaces were provided for the arrival of spaceships that were to take Ji and his faithful followers off to another planet. The spaceships failed to arrive, however, and, subsequently, Ji's membership fell to less than 10,000. With this caveat in mind, the Guru is fervently trying to make a comeback on the cult scene (Cameron, 1973).

A.C. Bhaktivedanta Swami Probhupada, the Indian who founded the International Society for Krishna Consciousness, was born in 1896. He was without question the absolute spiritual leader of Hare Krishna. From the best evidence I have, the movement will be in serious trouble because the venerable old Indian holy man recently died. This seems likely because without the charismatic leadership of the Swami, the Krishnas are left without a successor to the ancient and venerable Lord Krishna, the movement's Supreme Godhead.

Overall, the primary impediment to greater acceptance of the Hare Krishna by young people has been the seeming contradiction between Hindu religion and Western philosophy and religion. This is why some Hare Krishna observers claim that the cult is beginning to "clean up its act." For example, male Krishnas have put on wigs and wear suits and ties. Even though their clothing reflects the style of the 1950s, their new "front" seems to have made them more acceptable to the general public (Levine, 1974; Stoner and Parke,

1978). Perhaps the Hare Krishna cult may give up their strict vegetarian diet and their Eastern spiritual doctrine and no longer claim to be a "total way of life" (see Dāsī and Dāsī, 1973).

According to available evidence, Reverend Moon's Unification Church is peaking; the members have increased their financial strength, however. All this has taken place because of the mounting criticism and outraged cries from parents of Moonie children to "stop the madness of Moon's cult." Yet, it would be rash at this writing to conclude that Moon's Church will not, in time, face great difficulty because the Church has not directed its efforts at alleviating many of its members' personal problems; for example, providing its young members with "more acceptable" styles of married life. To this point, Moon's "strange brand" of Oriental monogamy has created disparity, when the preferred marriage for most of his American Moonies appears to be a wider range of choices with whom to marry or live with, not yet available within the social structure of Moon's Church (Culpepper, 1978; Sontag, 1977).

Since Moon's goal is to establish a worldwide benevolent theocracy, the question raised here is whether or not his followers will be able to pursue the Church's religious ideology with great passion, or will they in time shift their focus to more worldly problems?

While it may be true that some Moonies are better than others at "keeping the faith," it is not true that all of them, or even most of them, are maintaining their cult membership over several years. Many have not overcome their feelings of despair and disillusionment, and they have turned away from Moon's sacred mission. This is a serious problem that the Unification Church must confront. Meanwhile, there appears to be growing suspicion among observers that the Moonies use "mind controlling techniques" to convert members to the dogma of Moon's Church. These practices will continue to render the movement more vulnerable to outside criticism and attack. Moreover, when greater numbers of people believe that the movement's leaders are mainly interested in self-glorification or in accumulating great wealth, the word, no doubt, will rapidly spread that these tactics are inconsistent with the presumed values of the Church. The movement may in time lose momentum (Sontag, 1977).

It is interesting to speculate that many other contemporary religious cults face an even more uncertain future than Reverend Moon's Unification Church. This seems likely because an attraction to the new religions has not caught on with large numbers of young people, who at the present time seem to find these ultimate-meaning doctrines too unconventional as ways to seek salvation. This is especially true of the less known and less influential religious cults, who at the present time often deviate more from mainstream religion than their more well-known counterparts. For example, there are seemingly hundreds of smaller new religious movements, of an ideologically diverse nature, scattered about the United States and Canada. By and large these are more localized variants such as Love Israel's (Paul Erdman) Church of Armageddon, a Seattle-based religious cult that teaches converts to use LSD " to get closer to God." On the other hand, the new religions, such as Zen Buddhism, Alan Noonan's Messiah's World Crusade, and Prophet Steve Gaskin's The Farm, generally stress communal living and/or practice mysticism. They do not, however, seek members other than those who have been singled out as being distinctive in their interest in meditative ritual or who wish to benefit from communal living. They do not attempt to hold onto their members with the zeal that the Unification Church or Hare Krishna does.

The Future of Cults on the Changing American Scene

The genesis of the new religions came about as the postbeatnik bohemian culture took shape during the early 1960s. It was during this time that young people became steadily more committed to unconventional religious groups and their charismatic leaders. The overwhelming significance of this commitment is that an erosion of traditional religious practice took place. Nevertheless, there is now evidence suggesting that even if some young people became totally committed to a cult perspective, some of them turned out to be less ardent defenders of their religious cult lifestyle than have others (Swope, 1980). This observation may seem contradictory because exotic religious cults caught the attention of popular writers and it seemed that young people who joined cults were totally committed to the cult's ideals. Indeed, there have been many scholarly observers of the new religions who fundamentally disagree with popular conception of religious cults (Needleman and Baker, 1978). Nevertheless, most scholarly writers seem to agree that young religious seekers seem to have a new quest and a euphoric vision of a new and more perfect social order. This is the very antithesis of our highly industrialized society. All this suggests that the greater the young person's degree of commitment to these principles, the more the likelihood of great frustration when these goals fail to materialize. This dissatisfaction has centered chiefly on their belief that they are not accomplishing their mission. Just how these frustrations and feelings of despair are translated into direct action, necessary to obtain greater self-fulfillment, vary from one religious cult to another. Evidence suggests, however, that many cult members seem to be uncomfortable these days. Religious converts feel that their cult's religious values are shared by most other Americans less often these days. This alienation of many cult members from traditional society is expressed by their growing feeling that this is indeed a "sick society" and that the radical spiritual change they seek is too long overdue. Consistent with this dissatisfaction with American society, cultists are more sensitive to the perceived obstacles to their future outlook (Rothchild and Wolf, 1976).

In spite of these seemingly serious setbacks, young people are still being recruited for cult membership. At the moment, there are about 2 million young Americans involved in the new religions (Perlman and Havertat, 1974). Regardless of the present number of cult members, this phenomenon cannot easily be ignored. We might also expect nontraditional religions to flourish as a result of our poor economic situation.

There has been talk recently of a movement back to the more secure days of the 1950s, especially among young people, as one might expect. Does all this suggest that we will witness a move back to the status quo of the 1950s or does this imply that young people are picking up the threads of a cultural change from where those a generation ago left off. Regardless of which statement is correct, it does seem that the new religions are taking hold across America as fast as the number of dissatisfactions among young people multiply. But the cult movement appears to have its appeal mainly among young idealists because the cult's radical proposals for change are in effect a kind of intellectual and religious smorgasbord from which these young people are sampling these days.

A large proportion of minority youth assert that they would like to see a radical change in our fundamental institutions. Young blacks are more cynical and more critical of the greater society than are their more affluent white counterparts. Will minority youth, then, cling to their relatively more conservative religious beliefs, or will they eventually don cult robes and take up a cult lifestyles? At the present time it seems that minority youth are unlikely to become candidates for cult conversion (Smith, 1978; Washington, 1972).

Popular and empirical conceptions of religious cults seem to suggest that it would be questionable whether cults would appeal to young people in less troublesome times. Why have only a relatively small number of disillusioned young people defected traditional religion and sought membership in the new religions? Have most of today's young people realized that a cult's theology and its practices are far too unconventional for them? Have those who joined a religious cult, and who have managed somehow to leave on their own accord, done so before total commitment to their cult membership took place (Conway and Siegelman, 1978; Stoner and Parke, 1978). These are serious questions that need to be explored before a fuller understanding of religious cults is possible.

Since most religious movements change over time, how do cults continue to hold on to members who joined before significant religious belief and value change took place?" Even if the religious seeker's beliefs and goals do not seem to change, most cults do change. People who join particular religious cults, owing to a strong commitment to nontraditional religious ideology or to utopian goals, may not change their religious beliefs but still may continue their membership because they have friends in the cult or because the process of conversion succeeded in teaching them to value their cult peers. This is especially important if a cult contains followers, who after a time are not held primarily by the cult's religious teaching or ideology, but stay on for seemingly more pragmatic reasons. Cult members may not leave because they do not see other viable alternatives.

In order to attain a more fulfilling life, some young people have a continuing *need* for spiritual growth. The question still remains "why a need for nontraditional religion?" I will, of course, gain nothing by citing evidence that a different kind of religion is *needed* by many of today's young people unless I also examine the assumptions that underlie this spiritual quest. Some understanding of this *need* can be gained by insight gleaned from considering that the protest movements of the 1960s played an *avant-garde* role in the development of the present-day new religions. More by what they represented than by what they actually did, the politically oriented and spiritually oriented protest movements dramatically illustrated to young people that they had experienced a lack of personal control. I strongly suggest that at this time a lack of political and religious efficacy in America was felt. By becoming more involved many young people showed that they wanted to change society through self-reliance and greater control.

Because of the short lag between the onset of a period of political unrest and the new religions in America, I should stop and restate what I believe are the personal and social motives for this new religious ferment. I need to do this in order to discover what the current status of cult religion is and proceed from there to predict their future. Then, in order to avoid myopia in my understanding of present-day cult religion, I will briefly explore the ramifications of cults as various ways people seek to change their lifestyle and to move away from the status quo of traditional religion.

What could persuade young people to give up their comfortable habits and seek the austerity of cult religion? It now seems obvious that a sense of alienation from traditional religion and the major social institutions and the search for an identity that had roots in the strivings for a new spiritual reawakening are the important factors. The new religions promised for many to be an alternative to traditional religion as well as a way to turn aside from life's struggles.

Keep in mind that in understanding why some present-day cults seem to persist while others fail, there are at least three important factors to be considered: (a) the degree to which young people renounce or accept their parent's traditional religious beliefs, (b) the degree to which young people learn alternative ways to examine lifestyles and then go out to validate the consequences of their options; and (c) the degree to which today's charismatic religious leaders seem willing to "exploit" the seeming weakness they see in our society and use these weaknesses to recruit today's young people.

When one examines the new religions from these vantage points, there seem to be *signs* that some cults are peaking and others losing ground. This is true even though there are a few exotic cults that have all but disappeared or have failed temporarily to gain momentum. For example, many former members of People's Temple, the Divine Light Mission, and Berg's Children of God have for the most part gone underground. Nonetheless, many of these cults emerged with only moderate "success" in the first place. This generalization can be somewhat misleading when one considers a religious cult such as the Divine Light Mission because the Mission still has faithful followers who are trying to get the movement off the ground floor. On the other hand, when a religious movement is tightly organized on a national or international level (Transcendental Meditation, Hare Krishna, or the Unification Church, for example), disciples can move a great distance from secular role expectations or traditional religion and still be able to attract and sustain several thousands of followers. Smaller and more local variants on the cult theme, such as the "Garbage Eaters" or the Children of God, are less likely to survive long because they seem to clearly distinguished from both larger religious cults and traditional religion, however. They are also less likely to coexist with other religious groups or their general community.

Given the fact that we are now experiencing a "rise and fall" of religious movements in America, it seems clear that we need to know much more about what conditions produce "failure" for some religious cults while others thrive. Mayer N. Zald and Roberta Ash (1966) note that when a social movement requires great commitment from its members, and aims to change their lives, it is less susceptible to traditional pressure to change its values and goals. On the other hand, social movements with relatively specific goals are more likely to fail following the accomplishment of their major goals than those with very general or ill-defined goals. In this case "success" tends to preempt the movement's reasons for existence. A social movement may fail, or at least suffer a serious setback, because its legitimacy is discredited among its own members. Followers outgrow the movement's goals or they lose interest. Hence, a social movement such as Moon's Unification Church or the Hare Krishnas that aims at changing society may eventually have members that become tired of waiting for "success" and they subsequently defect in large numbers.

It is known that if a religious movement is to attract and sustain a large following it needs maintain an appealing theme or ideology and it has to seek a group of young idealists whose faith does not fade. This is usually accomplished through flamboyant gatherings of young people or small group interaction. Even though young religious seekers search for spiritual guidance from a religious cult, many eventually outgrow the challenge of a cult's authority they formerly accepted. This is not all happenstance because the very religion that promised to transform the young idealist's world into a "blissfully good fit" has been outgrown by the changes in the society it opposes and/or in the changes that have taken place in its membership.

Because a religious cult may have reached a high point in its development, due to conditions of social unrest, it often paradoxically has done so by first gaining some popularity with more established institutions (e.g., People's Temple). To this point, a nontraditional movement may suffer serious setbacks especially when things seem not to go well. If those who have formally given the movement legitimacy have now become critics of the movement they can "successfully" discredit it as a viable instrument for social change. In such cases it seems highly probable that what was at first a highly valued religious organization, where people acted in consort to accomplish certain goals, can become the object of great curiosity and criticism.

This is not the whole story because when a religious leader, who is worshipped by his followers for his prophecy of utopia, becomes strongly committed to this belief, followers may come to expect a perpetual life of bliss. Should the cult's messiah fall out of power with his followers, the cult is also likely to fall. Reverend Jim Jones' People's Temple seems to underscore this very point. Jones' search for utopia in his rain forest "paradise" was doomed to fail because many of his followers, no doubt, obeyed him more out of fear than loyalty. The whole religious cult came down when Jones failed to keep pace with his followers' basic human needs. Ostensibly, under more ideal conditions they could be deprived by pretense and still continue to privately and publicly accept his utopian plan for their salvation. But the jungle *Götterdämmerung*, propitiated by Jim Jones, fulfilled his religious cult's apocalyptic dream only by a tragic massacre-suicide (Lincoln and Mamiya, 1980).

What Has Been Done to Stop the New Religions?

What can be done to stem the tide of cults? Can the courts stop young people from joining a cult or does the answer lie with traditional religion? Carroll Stoner and Jo Anne Parke (1978) propose that we could formulate and pass laws prohibiting religious cults from proselytizing on public school grounds or on college campuses. They tell us that cities can develop zoning laws, such as the legislation passed in Evanston, Illinois. The Evanston City Legislature forced local Krishnas to remain in their own immediate community, prohibiting them from recruiting or selling their books elsewhere.

Are there other ways cults can be controlled? Stoner and Parke suggest that the federal government could make sure that cults do not violate the Internal Revenue Service codes nor our immigration and naturalization laws. They reason that since many religious cult leaders immigrate to the United States to set up their religious movements their passports and visas could be inspected.

Before the reader takes Stoner's and Parke's suggestions seriously, he or she should realize that state and federal appellate court decisions support the religious freedom of cult leaders and their converts. The *United States* v. *Seeger* decision (1965), involving conscientious objectors, states that courts cannot question the sincerity of a person's religious beliefs, because our federal laws do in fact guarantee an individual's basic constitutional right to freedom of religion, speech, association, and privacy. Of course, broadly conceived, this right extends to cult leaders who are here in order to establish their religious movements.

Now what about the reaction to religious cults by established churches? In recent years there have been an increasing number of attempts by traditional churches to prevent cults from recruiting their young people. In this respect, religious cult leaders seem to have made traditional religious leaders uncomfortable. Some traditionalists are now doing some serious "soul searching," asking why young people are leaving their churches for cults in such alarming numbers (Enroth, 1979). It is worth noting here that the "rigid compartmentalization" of religious dogma and practice has not satisfied both the demands of the young church member's personal needs nor do many young people these days subscribe to the credo that mainstream churches should only be concerned with the traditional role of spreading God's word. The most striking consequence of this reaction is that many young people are now coming to recognize that they are less likely to find self-fulfillment or spiritual growth within their traditional church. Many of today's youth are caught up in a seemingly acute dilemma because they are not experiencing satisfying personal relationships and they have not found a new lifestyle through membership in a traditional church. This is why some religious scholars argue that religious cults represent, on one level, strategies for making sense out of the current state of moral and ethical relativism. Many young people have not found in more traditional religious settings the kind of spiritual and personal satisfaction they are seeking. According to this view, established religion has created its own crises by raising eschatological expectations without at the same time satisfying members' personal and social needs (Enroth, 1979; Needleman and Baker, 1978).

Cults are diverse; traditional religion is homogeneous. For example, Will Herberg (1965) tells us that the doctrinal differences among the three major American faiths (Protestantism, Catholicism, Judaism) is declining in favor of an emerging consensus on fundamental religious issues. This has taken place in spite of some current sect movements, such as the Pentecostal and Holiness sects. Nevertheless, these sect movements are considered too minor to seriously challenge conventional religious theology and practice.

One characteristic of the three major faiths is that they generally do not encourage great lay participation in their religious ceremonies, whereas most of the new religions, and especially cults, are basically religions where member participation is at a high level. Incidentally, there is indirect evidence suggesting that religions that encourage great involvement in their ritual and dogma tend to have members who hold more intense and devout religious beliefs than those that do not encourage these practices (Kephart, 1976). This observation is consistent with my view that strong behavioral commitment is a necessary condition to connect people's religious beliefs to their dogma and practice (Yinger, 1970).

What about the children of cult members who are forced by their parents to live with them in a cult setting? Will they grow up and accept their parent's cult lifestyle or will they, in spite of their parents, turn to the rejected traditional religion of their parents? There is a valuable lesson to be learned if we collect longitudinal data on what has happened to children born into a cult setting. If this were done, I fear the data would suggest that these young children may break all ties with conventional aspects of society. Many things may go wrong with their lives. Perhaps the most telling evidence might be that their disillusionment has deepened into despair. They may even, more than their cult parents, hold the general belief that the American social system is morally bankrupt, evil, and unredeemable. This negative view may be only part of their problem; they may not come to see any viable alternative to their cult identity and lifestyle. In a sense, then, have cult children anticipated their own disappointment? Will this result in a marked drop in their self-esteem and self-worth? They, no doubt, have been socialized to expect the good life and they may come to find out that their religious cause and their desire to change society has only enhanced their frustration (Stoner and Parke, 1979).

Despite the grim litany of opposition to religious cults, it should be remembered that bitterness seems to run deepest where it is most personal. This is what prompts me to ask: "What happens to those who choose to leave their cult life behind?" Can these people eventually return to the more conventional aspects of society, or will most of them turn to yet another cult or to drugs and alcohol as they carry the stigma of their former cult life? Ex-cultists will have to confront the upheavals and personal threats to living in what they formerly construed as a hostile noncult world. Changes away from a cult lifestyle are likely to signal the end of a strong cult identity and dependence on the cult's "rigid" norms. I would predict that the more unconventional and dogmatic the convert's beliefs and practices before defecting, the more difficult the change to a non-cult identity.

These observations suggest that the implications for a postcult life are staggering. The young idealist will have to give up a great measure of privacy and let others penetrate his or her life. Cult members have been socialized to think that they are special and their values and beliefs are more deeply planted than they may even come to realize. So it seems that the young converts are socialized not to live in the noncult world. Perhaps the greatest incapacity of all may be the inability of converts to put their cult life in the past in order to function in the greater society. To this extent it is now known that many ex-cultists (those who have been studied) still are plagued by the transition back to a noncult lifestyle. At best, these former cult devotees are continuing to explore their alternatives out of what their parents considered a quagmire (Singer, 1979).

I have cited some writers who have depicted cults in a negative way exclusively. They have paid little attention to the role cults play in bringing about positive change in members. I should say that a few religious scholars do not view all cultists as victims of a cult leader's dream for utopia. They claim that young converts are generally responsible youth taking positive action on their misfor-tunes to change their future for the better (Needleman and Baker, 1978). Unfortunately this relatively positive characterization of present-day cultists seems to be the exception rather than the rule. This is, no doubt, why many young cult people have prompted negative reactions from their noncult world (Stoner and Parke, 1978). Indirect evidence for this interpretation comes from research done on Lerner's *just world hypothesis* (Lerner and Miller, 1978). This hypothesis suggests that people have a strong need to believe that the world is a fair and equitable place, where "goodness triumphs over evil." People tend to believe that those who violate society's norms will be punished sooner or later and that those who are unjustly punished will be compensated in the long run. What follows from Lerner's theory is that people are likely to believe that young cultists bring about their own misfortune; they caused their own unhappiness because they are the kind of people who deserve what they get out of life. This is what makes it possible for people to continue to view their world as just, despite the seemingly strong evidence that young cultists suffer from an identity crisis and alienation from society's major institutions. Elaine Walster (1966) notes that many people do not even want to believe that others suffer negative outcomes without first assuming that they have negative personality characteristics that caused their misfortune. People who are hurt, suffering from low self-esteem, or otherwise alienated from society's major institutions do seem to need close supportive relationships. To this point, there is evidence showing that intimate social relations with similar others lessens the impact of a troublesome life (Wortman and Silver, 1980).

I should hasten to stress that the last word on cults is not likely to be written because the miracles and superhuman powers ascribed to cult leaders by their devotees are part of the flamboyant curiosity that young devotees tend to show for their messiah or guru. These leaders are often religious charismatics against which one finds little to weigh except their shadowy claim to save mankind. Yet the shadow can become a massive and destructive force because we have not yet reached the end of the road chartered by cult leaders such as Charles Manson and Jim Jones. Throughout the changing of time and events the dilemma persists. Even though cult leaders come and go, and their influence and their religious dogma and practice seem on the surface different, they still, under the proper circumstances, can produce no less than devastating outcomes for their youthful followers.

Finally, a seminal question to ask is whether or not both the Eastern and Western cult persuasions will persist in America over a relatively long time? A yes answer is justified to some degree because the social and personal conditions necessary for these religious cults' ferments have become increasingly more difficult to abate. I am afraid this is true because many of today's young idealistic religious seekers are still plagued by transient feelings of dissatisfaction with our basic social institutions. Hence, the ripple set in motion by the new religions is not likely to stop (Enroth, 1979).

A Postscript on
the New Religious Cults

My search for an understanding of religious cults continues, as perhaps any inquiry must, and there are a number of observations that necessitate my making some final comments.

I distinguished between traditional religion and cult religion on the basis of several criteria. I also began with a definition of religious cults that places them in the context of the new religions and differentiates them from sects. When I did this I suggested that religious cults are at best only marginally accepted as alternatives to traditional religion. Perhaps this is why only a relatively small number of today's youthful religious seekers have become totally converted to cult religion. To this point, I noted that cult religious seekers are often labeled deviant because they are not generally accorded a legitimate status by traditionally established religious leaders nor have they been considered psychologically wholesome by many psychologists, psychiatrists, popular writers, and members of the mass media.

I have shown that some writers have considered, for the most part, that young cult devotees are themselves psychologically disturbed. I also noted, however, that this is but one image of young cultists that we can compose out of many. For instance, the religious cult finds the young religious seekers at a time of need; when the promise for belonging to an accepting group seems an attractive way to gain a new and more positive identity. Once young idealists join a religious cult, however, they often find that the intense display of love and acceptance ("love bombing") is followed by an isolation from their former world. The demands made on them — hard work, discipline, and the group's practice of ritual — all tend to make it increasingly more unlikely that premies can emotionally and intellectually resist overcommitment to the religious cult. This process is often facilitated by demanding that converts sign over their worldly belongings to the cult and devote full time to the cult's mission. The young premies must acknowledge former sins and then show that they have a strong need for a cult redemption. Because of the young identity seekers' desire for social acceptance and approval, they develop a strong bond to the cult group. There are pressures to totally accept the cult leader's doctrine and plans for utopia. Even if converts should decide to leave their cult peers, guilt and an intense sense of loyalty are likely to prevent this. A childlike dependency on the group and its leader develops. At this point, young people find it difficult or almost impossible to leave the group; their commitment to the group is too firm and their former value systems have been replaced by that of the cult. As time goes by, and the more the cult demands personal sacrifice, the greater the value converts place on cult membership. It is in this sense that premies have validated their commitment to their religious choice.

I demonstrated that cult leaders are charismatics who establish credibility with their followers through claims of faith healing and stylistic ritual. They are perceived as the personal savior of their followers and are often attributed godlike characteristics. But once young idealists are *totally converted* to the leader's dogma, they tend to embrace, internalize, and act on their leader's conceptions of reality. Then, clearly, their designations of themselves as a sinner, inadequate, and demoralized can act to support their leader's claim that they can be saved through a special cult redemption for their presumed former sins.

As simple as the message sounds, what I have suggested is that those who join religious cults are likely to be judged deviant by their former community and therefore deemed undesirable. Then, in a surprising twist of logic, as young people disclose their need for a spiritual reawakening and their disillusionment with our major social institutions and establish a close bond with similar others, they become vulnerable to stigma and stereotypical images (Glick et al., 1974; Wortman and Silver, 1980). Learning to give oneself to a cult means rejecting many old ideas about what constitutes social reality. This is why I have suggested that one way to understand young religious seekers is to understand that they have been converted to a cult lifestyle and have formed a different self-identity that is at odds with the greater society's expectations.

In my sojourn through the new religions, I noted that religious cults grew out of the efforts of religious seekers, particularly young idealists, to look for a more rewarding spiritual life and a new identity. Present-day cults have also been a part of a more general movement toward a spiritual reawakening initiated in the 1960s, for the most part by self-styled charismatic religious leaders. These leaders drew their converts from the once complacent middle-class religious seekers of orthodox religions who were disillusioned by and alienated from their parents' religion and society's major institutions.

Because of our lack of knowledge about conditions underlying different religious cults, I have considered them as a generic and undoubtedly dramatic phenomenon. Just how we translate this into a concern for how the followers of Eastern religious cults are different from these new religions indigenous to America is yet to be demonstrated in the literature. To this point, followers of the Eastern cults (Hare Krishna or the Divine Light Mission, for example) seem more intellectual and more oriented toward personal or inner spiritual development and they seem to attract the more academically competent than indigenously American cults, such as the Children of God or Scientology. Regardless of whether a religious cult has had an Eastern or Western origin, its religious cult leader promises followers a rewarding life and a chance to save humanity from what is perceived as sin and corruption. This requires that religious seekers make great sacrifices for their cult membership. This is made easy because they are taught that they are part of an elite group, morally and ethically superior to people who are not part of their religious movement. This means that young idealists must remove themselves from their former community by turning away from their family, school, and work. This is deemed necessary in order to prove that one is worthy in the eyes of the cult.

Religious seekers are taught to accept, without question, their leader's religious doctrine and program for a more perfect society. In order to expedite this plan, premies are provided with a sample of what utopia might be like: Ready-made friendships and "love bombing" from one's peers takes place as these idealists share a common mission and set of religious beliefs and values. This activity tends to increase the premies' commitment to their cult. However, commitment to a cult lifestyle deepens if young idealists experience a *turning point* and becomes *totally converted.* When this happens many cultists eventually come to pronounce society wrong and consequently find it difficult to return to their former world. As they continue to explore their consciousness, they feel compelled to denounce traditional career and family plans because they feel that the society that offered them these options no longer is morally worthy of participation. The cult teaches them that only one's fellow members are to be trusted. They share a common belief that society is decadent and morally bankrupt.

Unfortunately, some young converts confront a future that is downright discouraging. Evidence suggests that many young religious seekers suffer from self-depreciation. To this point, clinical interviews with ex-cultists show that they often exhibit self-defeating behavior that can be quite costly to their future. Provided with an escape from society, young idealists increase the likelihood of stereotypical labeling. Parents of young cult converts seem surprised—even shocked—when they hear their child has joined one. This is caused, in part, by the mass media and popular writers who report that religious cults recruit members through the use of guilt, manipulation, isolation, fear, deception, and strong demands for public displays of commitment to the cult's lifestyle. Some writers have even claimed that these techniques are not unlike those used in "brainwashing." Young idealists are said to be especially vulnerable because they often are said to suffer from identity problems, mild depression, indecision, and alienation from their family, peers, and childhood religion.

As religious cults caught the attention of the mass media, many of their members discovered that their charismatic leader's vision of utopia turned out to be quite different from what they were led into believing. This was not unexpected because cult leaders formulate their group's religious dogma, and in order to hold on to their followers, they must assume a position of absolute authority. What are the implications of a cult lifestyle as a total way of life? The contradictions I have noted are not always readily apparent to the young convert. They are either glossed over or treated too lightly as the premie turns away from career and family goals and accepts the cult's plans for a more perfect society. Unlike most other religious groups, religious cults are not open to public accountability. Even the young converts generally lack any participation in the cult's decision-making processes. This is because the cult's leaders secretly manage their cult's affairs in order to create a feeling that "all is well." As long as the cult does not confront a crisis or a serious setback, the premies may never discover the contradiction between their cult lifestyle and the dismal prospects for their future. Then, in a real sense, many young converts have anticipated the disappointment of their moral and spiritual expectations. They have been taught to expect the good life. The awesome consequences of their cult membership makes some former cult members feel uncomfortable when they learn that there is no foolproof prescription for happiness. This was promised by the cult leader, who by any standard is difficult to impugn or to fulminate. This is why it is difficult for me to see how many young idealists can avoid being caught up in the vortex of forces that surrounds the religious cult.

We often consider youth special: they are generally considered innocent, dependent, and, because of their presumed immaturity, not wholly responsible for their actions. Nonetheless, the public's mystification of religious cults is not without its powerful negative effects. The public's stereotypical reactions to converts as deviant religious seekers has affected their protracted negative view of the world in such self-fulfilling ways that they are likely to continue to substantiate the presumed validity of these negative characterizations. This is why I believe that these young idealists unwittingly anticipate their own shortcomings. The road back to society's expectations will be replete with problems of readjustment for many of these youths. This view is underscored by reports that deprogrammers and clinicians have all too often failed to achieve their purpose of "successfully deconverting" former converts. They often slip back into the fold of their former cult, or are left with transient feelings of guilt and anxiety.

When I look toward the relatively distant future, then, I anticipate that there will be a continuing youthful search for a positive self-image and identity and a new spiritual sensibility based upon the best of today's and tomorrow's worlds. Society's norms and values are changing, and as what young people want out of life becomes even more clearly articulated than today, my hope for their future is that today's lessons will serve as a lesson for tomorrow's youth. They, no doubt, will be as idealistically focused on their future as are today's young religious seekers.

Glossary

Altered States of Consciousness. Where the cultists feel that there has been a qualitative change in the pattern of mental functioning away from the "normal" waking state of experiencing consciousness.

Ashram. The cult's retreat or domicile.

Attribution. Inferring that someone has a particular characteristic or trait on the basis of observing something about the person's behavior.

Attitude. The intensity of positive or negative affect or feeling for or against an object.

Authoritarianism. A basic personality style that includes a set of organized beliefs, values, and preferences, including submission to authority, identification with authority, etc.

Bhagavad-Gita. The sacred Hindu text written in Vedic or Sanskrit studied by Hare Krishna devotees; the claim is that Vedic knowledge is necessary to know Krishna.

Blissed Out. A condition of apparent apathy owing to "excessive" meditation and/or chanting.

"Brainwashing" Intensive and often prolonged forms of propaganda conducted under conditions of isolation and stress; designed to induce great changes in thinking or personality; a term derived from Korean POW experience.

Charisma. A personal attribute assumed to be possessed by certain leaders that tends to "draw" or elicit support and admiration from others.

Charismatic Leader. Authority based on followers' intense positive feelings for their leader; authority based on the individual rather than the process by which the person obtained a leadership role.

Civil Religion. Where the role of religion is used to evaluate moral and ethical principles from a political point of view; for example, Reverend Moon's Unification Church.

Coersive Persuasion. Techniques of indoctrination used to obtain compliance and conformity to the group's standards (norms).

Cognitive Dissonance. An unpleasant emotional state, somewhat like anxiety, tension, or unease, which is induced whenever a person experiences inconsistency between his or her attitudes, or between his or her attitudes and behavior.

Commitment. A process by which a person adheres to normative behaviors because disruptive consequences of not conforming would interfere with the attainment of one's ends or values.

Credibility. The perceived expertise and trustworthiness of a leader (or communicator). The more expert and trustworthy the person, the greater his or her credibility.

Cult. A religious group, lead by a charismatic messiah or guru, whose beliefs and practices are deviant from traditional religion and from mainstream society.

Cult Proselytization. How cultists gain the attention of prospects and how cults promote acceptance of their religious doctrine.

Deprogramming. Techniques used to deconvert cult members; generally includes isolation from others, systematic questioning of any support the person expresses for the cult, ridicule, and deprivation of food and sleep.

Doomsday Cult. A religious group with a messiah or guru who predicts the end of an era or the world; only devotees can be saved.

E-Meter. A special psycho-galvanometer used by Scientologists to measure what is going on physiologically during a confrontation between the cult member and the "auditor" when measures of engrams (scars) are being erased; actually an apparatus used to measure changes in electrical conductivity of, or activity in, the skin; reactions are taken as indicators of emotional reactivity.

Floating. Where the cultist, who is attempting to leave a cult life behind, experiences a flashback or returns symbolically to the cult and may even think he or she hears exhortations from the cult leader or former cult peers.

Foot-in-the-Door Technique. The compliance strategy in which a small request is made first and is then followed by a larger one.

Group Cohesiveness. A central property of groups relating to the degree to which members of the group are attracted to the group and desire to remain part of it.

Group-Polarization Effect. Refers to the fact that following group discussion, individuals often shift toward views that are more extreme than the ones they initially supported.

Guru. A charismatic religious teacher or guide or leader (the venerable one); from Hindu religion.

Heavenly Deception. A technique used by cultists to sell their books or wares to unwitting buyers; lies and deceptions are justified as necessary to "spread the word."

Karma. The "soul" or "life matter" that inhabits all living things according to Hindu religious doctrine.

Krishna. The supreme Godhead of Hindu religion through which Vedic knowledge is said to flow.

Leader. That member of a group who exercises the greatest amount of influence and authority over others.

Love Bombing. The "excessive" degree of "love and affection" shown new recruits or cult premies.

Mantra Meditation. A sound pattern that is meditated on; In Transcendental Meditation, syllables drawn from the Hindu holy books that are silently chanted by meditators, who exclude all other thoughts from their minds.

Millenarian Movement. A movement in which the imminence of a radical and supernatural change in the social order is prophesied or expected, so as to lead to organization and activity, carried out in preparation for this event; for example, a doomsday cult.

Natural High. A feeling of elation brought about without drugs, generally through the practice of meditation.

Norm. An implicitly or explicitly agreed upon standard of behavior; an expectation shared by members of a group about how one should behave.

Obedience. Conforming to direct orders from a high-status person.

Objective Self-Awareness. A cognitive state in which attention is focused inward on the self.

Pikarume. (Blood cleansing) A religious practice of the Unification Church where the original sin of Eve is "purified" through marriage to a man chosen by Reverend Moon.

Premie. A reborn person or a convert or cult devotee.

Reference Group. The group used by an individual as the standard against which to evaluate oneself.

Satsang. Reinforcement of a religious belief through meditation or discussion.

Sect. An informal religious group; membership is through conversion; services are highly emotional and entail a great deal of religious ritual and participation; often a splintering off from a mainstream religion.

Self-Perception Theory. The view that people often infer their attitudes, emotions, and other internal states partly from observations of their own behavior and the circumstances under which it occurs.

Sensory Deprivation. Sensory stimulation well below the "normal" level of sensory input; achieved by reducing visual, auditory, and other sensory areas of stimulation; often leads to hallucinations and delusions.

Social Comparison. A basic drive to evaluate one's own opinions and abilities, which in turn leads to comparisons between oneself and other people.

Social Movement. A conscious, collective, or organized attempt to bring about change (or resist change) on a large scale; the change is directed at the social order through noninstitutionalized means.

Social Reality. The world as defined by humans.

Swami. A Hindu religious title of respect; a Hindu religious teacher or leader.

Total Environment. The creation of an environment in which rewards and punishments are controlled by the group's members.

Yogi. One who practices yoga; a religious teacher or leader.

References

Alland, A. (1962) Possession in revivalistic Negro church. *Journal for the Scientific Study of Religion,* 1:204-213.

Aronson, E., and Mills, J. (1959) Effect of severity of initiation on liking for a group. *Journal of Abnormal and Social Psychology,* 59:177-181.

Asch, S. E. (1956) Studies of independence and conformity: A minority of one against a unanimous majority. *Psychological Monographs,* 7 (No. 9) (Whole No. 416).

Back, K. W. (1973) *Beyond Words: The Story of Sensitivity Training and the Encounter Movement.* Baltimore, MD: Penguin Books.

Back, K. W. et al. (1977) *Social Psychology.* New York: John Wiley.

Bales, R. F. (1976) *Personality and Interpersonal Behavior.* New York: Holt, Rinehart & Winston.

Barber, B. (1941) Acculturation and messianic movements. *American Sociological Review,* 6:663-669.

Batson, D. (1976) Moon madness: Greed or creed? *American Psychological Association Monitor,* 7 (No. 6):1, 32.

Beir, E. G., and Valens, E. G. (1975) *People Reading.* New York: Warner Books.

Bellah, R. N. (1967) Civil religion in America. *Daedalus,* 96:1-21.

Bem, D. J. (1972) Self-perception theory. In L. Berkowitz (Ed.), *Advances in Experimental Social Psychology* (Vol. 6). New York: Academic Press.

Bem, D. J., and Allen, A. (1974) On predicting some of the people some of the time. The search for cross-situational consistencies in behavior. *Psychological Review,* 81:506-520.

Berscheid, E., and Walster, E. H. (1978) *Interpersonal Attraction*, 2nd ed. Reading, MA: Addison-Wesley.

Bird, F. (1978) Charisma and ritual in new religious movements. In J. Needleman and G. Baker (Eds.), *Understanding the New Religions*. New York: The Seabury Press.

Blank, T. O. (1978) Two social psychologies: Is segregation inevitable? *Personality and Social Psychology Bulletin*, 4:553-556.

Blumer, H. (1969) Collective behavior. In A. McClung Lee et al. (Eds.), *Principles of Sociology*, 3rd. ed. New York: Barnes and Noble.

Bolt, M. (1975) Purpose of life and religious orientation. *Journal of Psychology and Theology*, 3:116-118.

Bowers, K. S. (1973) Situationism in psychology: An analysis and critique. *Psychological Review*, 80:307-336.

Braden, C. S. (1970) *These Also Believe: A Study of Modern American Cults and Minority Religious Movement*. New York: Macmillan.

Brewer, M. (1975) We're gonna tear you down and put you back together. *Psychology Today*, 8:39.

Brickman, P. (1969) Attitudes out of context: Harvard students go home. Undergraduate Honors Thesis, Harvard University, 1964. Reported in K. Gergan, *The Psychology of Behavior Exchange*. Reading, MA: Addison-Wesley, pp. 2-5.

Briggs, D. C. (1970) *Your Child's Self-Esteem: The Key to His Life*. New York: Doubleday.

Bronfenbrenner, U. (1970) *Two Worlds of Childhood: U.S. and U.S.S.R.* New York: Russell Sage.

Bugliosi, V., and Gentry, C. (1975) *Helter Skelter*. New York: Bantam Books.

Burham, K. (1963). Father Divine: A case study of charismatic leadership. Ph.D. dissertation, University of Pennsylvania.

Buys, C. (1978) Humans would do better without groups. *Personality and Social Psychology Bulletin*, 4:123-125.

Byrne, D. (1971) *The Attraction Paradigm*. New York: Academic Press.

Cameron, C. (Ed.). (1973) *Who Is Guru Maharaj Ji?* New York: Bantam Books.

Campbell, D. T. (1957) Factors relevant to validity of experiments in social settings. *Psychological Bulletin*, 54:297-312.

Cantril, H. (1969) The kingdom of Father Divine. In B. McLaughlin (Ed.)., *Studies in Social Movements: A Social Psychological Perspective*. New York: The Free Press, pp. 223-242.

Cantril, H., and Sherif, M. (1938) Kingdom of Father Divine. *Journal of Abnormal Psychology*, 33:147-167.

Carlsmith, J. M., Ellsworth, P. C., and Aronson, E. (1976) *Methods of Research in Social Psychology*. Reading, MA: Addison-Wesley.

Clark, R., and Sechrest, L. (1976) The mandate phenomenon. *Journal of Personality and Social Psychology*, 34:1057-1061.

Cohen, D. (1975) *The New Believers*. New York: M. Evans, Inc.

Conway, F., and Siegelman, J. (1978) *Snapping*. Philadelphia, PA: Lippincott.

Cox, H. (1978) Deep structures in the study of new religions. In J. Needleman and G. Baker (Eds.). *Understanding the New Religions*. New York: The Seabury Press.

Crandall, J. E., and Rasmussen, R. D. (1975) Purpose in life as related to specific values. *Journal of Clinical Psychology*, 31:433-435.

Crumbaugh, J. C., and Maholick, L. T. (1969) *The Purpose in Life Test*. Munster, ID: Psychometric Affiliates.

Culpepper, E. (1978) The spiritual movement of radical feminist consciousness. In J. Needleman and G. Baker (Eds.), *Understanding the New Religions*. New York: The Seabury Press.

Darley, J. M., and Darley, S. A. (1976) Conformity and deviation. In J. W. Thibaut et al. (Eds.), *Contemporary Topics in Social Psychology*. Morristown, NJ: General Learning Press.

Dāsī, Krishna Devī, and Dāsī, Sama Devī. (1973) *The Hare Krishna Cookbook*. Radnor, PA: Chilton.

Davis, J. H. (1969) *Group Performance*. Reading, MA: Addison-Wesley.

Dion, K. L. (1973) Cohesiveness as a determinant of in-group outgroup bias. *Journal of Personality and Social Psychology*, 28:163-171.

Dittes, J. E. (1969) Psychology of religion. In G. Lindzey and E. Aronson (Eds.), *The Handbook of Social Psychology* (Vol. 5). Reading, MA: Addison-Wesley.

Dohrman, H. T. (1958) *California Cult*. Boston, MA: Beacon Press.

Doress, I., and Porter, J. N. (1978) *Kids in Cults. Society*, 15:69-71.

Duval, S., and Wicklund, R. A. (1972) *A Theory of Objective Self-Awareness*. New York: Academic Press.

Edwards, C. (1978) *Crazy for God: The Nightmare of Cult Life*. New York: The Seabury Press.

Endler, N. S., and Magnusson, D. (1976) *Interactional Psychology and Personality*. New York: Halsted Press.

Enroth, R. (1979) *The Lure of Cults*. New York: Christian Herald Books.

Erikson, E. H. (1968) *Identity, Youth and Crisis*. New York: Norton.

Fabry, J. B. (1968) *The Pursuit of Meaning: Logotherapy Applied to Life*. Boston, MA: Beacon Press.

Festinger, L. A. (1954) Theory of social comparison processes. *Human Relations*, 7:117-140.

Festinger, L. A., Riecken, H. W., and Schachter, S. (1956) *When Prophecy Fails: A Social and Psychological Study of a Modern Group That Predicted the Destruction of the World*. New York: Harper.

Fiedler, F. E. (1971) *Leadership*. New York: General Learning Press.

Fishbein, M., and Ajzen, I. (1975) *Belief, Attitude, Intention and Behavior*. Reading, MA: Addison-Wesley.

Freedman, J. L., and Doob, A. (1968) *Deviancy: The Psychology of Being Different*. New York: Academic Press.

Freedman, J. L., and Fraser, S. C. (1966) Compliance without pressure: The foot-in-the-door technique. *Journal of Personality and Social Psychology*, 4:195-202.

French, J.R.P., Jr., and Raven, B. (1959) The bases of social power. In D. Cartwright (Ed.), *Studies in Social Power*. Ann Arbor, MI: University of Michigan Press.

Freud, S. (1950) A religious experience. *Collected Papers* (Vol. V). London: Hogarth Press.

Frieze, I. H., and Bar-Tal, D. (1979) Attribution theory: Past and present. In I. H. Frieze, D. Bar-Tal, and J. S. Carroll (Eds.), *New Approaches to Social Problems*. San Francisco: Jossey-Bass.

Garrison, O. V. (1974) *The Hidden Story of Scientology*. Secaucus, NJ: Citadel Press.

Gerard, H. B., and Mathewson, G. C. (1966) The effects of severity of interaction on liking for a group: A replication. *Journal of Experimental Social Psychology*, 2:278-287.

Gerrard, N. (1971) The serpent-handling religions of West Virginia. In I. L. Horowitz and M. S. Strong (Eds.), *Sociological Realities*. New York: Harper & Row.

Gibb, C. A. (1969) Leadership. In G. Lindzey and E. Aronson (Eds.), *Handbook of Social Psychology*. Vol. 4, 2nd ed. Reading, MA: Addison-Wesley, pp. 205-282.

Gibbons, D. C., and Jones, J. F. (1975) *The Study of Deviance: Perspectives and Problems*. Englewood Cliffs, NJ: Prentice-Hall.

Glick, I. O., Weiss, R. S., and Parkes, C. M. (1974) *The First Years of Bereavement*. New York: John Wiley.

Glock, C. Y., and Stark, R. (1962) *Religion and Society in Tension*. Chicago: Rand McNally.

Goffman, E. (1971) *Relations in Public*. New York: Harper & Row.

Goleman, D. (1978) The impact of the new religions on psychology. In J. Needleman and G. Baker (Eds.), *Understanding the New Religions*. New York: The Seabury Press, pp. 113-121.

Grove, W. R. (1970) Societal reaction as an explanation of mental illness: An evaluation. *American Sociological Review*, 35:873-884.

Gurwitz, S. B., and Topol, B. (1978) Determinants of confirming and disconfirming responses to negative social labels. *Journal of Experimental Social Psychology*, 14:31-42.

Guten, S. (1978) Deviant identity formation: A social psychological synthesis. In S. D. Feldman (Ed.), *Deciphering Deviance*. Boston, MA: Little, Brown.

Harder, M. W., Richardson, J. T., and Simmonds, R. B. (1976-77) Jesus people. In D. Krebs (Ed.), *Readings in Social Psychology: Contemporary Perspectives* (1976-77 ed.). New York: Harper & Row.

Hardyck, J. A., and Braden, M. (1962) Prophecy fails again: A report of a failure to replicate. *Journal of Abnormal and Social Psychology*, 65:136-141.

Herberg, W. (1965) *Protestant-Catholic-Jew*. Garden City, NY: Doubleday.

Hoffer, E. (1951) *The True Believer*. New York: Harper.

Hollander, E. P. (1976) *Principles and Methods of Social Psychology*, 3rd ed. New York: Oxford University Press.

Hollander, E. P., and Julian, J. W. (1969) Contemporary trends in the analysis of leadership processes. *Psychological Bulletin*, 71:387-397.

Homans, G. C. (1974) *Social Behavior: Its Elementary Forms*, rev. ed. New York: Harcourt Brace Jovanovich.

Hood, R. W., Jr. (1975) The construction and preliminary validation of a measure of reported mystical experience. *Journal for the Scientific Study of Religion*, 14:29-41.

Hopkins, J. M. (1978) The children of God: New revelations. *Christianity Today*, 22:44.

— — —., (1980) The children of God: Fewer far out. *Christianity Today*, 24:40-41.

Hubbard, L.R.R. (1972) *Dianetics: The Modern Science of Mental Health*. Los Angeles: Publications Organization.

Jabes, J. (1978) *Individual Processes in Groups and Organizations*. Arlington Heights, IL: AHM Publishing Corporation.

James, W. (1902) *The Varieties of Religious Experience*. New York: The Modern Library.

Jones, E. E., and Nisbett, R. E. (1971) The actor and the observer: Divergent perceptions of the causes of behavior. In E. E. Jones et al. (Eds.), *Attribution: Perceiving the causes of behavior*. Morristown, NJ: General Learning Press.

Jones, R. A., Hendrich, C., and Epstein, Y. M. (1979) *Introduction to Social Psychology*. Sunderland, MA: Sinaner Associates.

Judah, J. S. (1978) New religions and religious liberty. In J. Needleman and G. Baker (Eds.), *Understanding the New Religions*. New York: The Seabury Press.

Kanter, R. M. (1972) *Commitment and Community: Communes and Utopias in Sociological Perspective*. Cambridge, MA: Harvard University Press.

Kelley, D. (1972) *Why Conservative Churches Are Growing*. New York: Harper & Row.

Kelley, H. H. (1952) Attitudes and judgments as influenced by reference groups: Two functions of reference groups. In G. Swanson, T. M. Newcomb, and E. L. Hartley (Eds.), *Readings in Social Psychology*, 2nd ed. New York: Holt, Rinehart and Winston, pp. 410-420.

Kephart, W. M. (1978) *Extraordinary Groups: The Sociology of Unconventional Life Styles*. New York: St. Martin's Press.

Kiesler, C. A. (1971) *The Psychology of Commitment: Experiments Linking Behavior to Belief*. New York: Academic Press.

Kiesler, C. A., and Sakumura, J. (1966) A test of a model for commitment. *Journal of Personality and Social Psychology*, 3:349-353.

Kiesler, S. (1978) *Interpersonal Processes in Groups and Organizations*. Arlington Heights, ILL: AHM Publishing Corporation.

Kildahl, J. P. (1965) The personalities of sudden religious converts. *Pastoral Psychology*, 16:37-44.

Kilduff, M., and Javers, R. (1978) *The Suicide Cult: The Inside Story of the People's Temple Sect and the Massacre in Guyana*. New York: Bantam Books.

Kim, Y. D. (1968) *Divine Principle and Its Application*. Washington, DC, The Holy Spirit Association for Unification of World Christianity.

Kleinke, C. L. (1978) *Self-Perception: The Psychology of Personal Awareness*. San Francisco: W. H. Freeman.

Krause, C. A. (1978) *Guyana Massacre: The Eyewitness Account*. New York: Berkley Publishing Corp.

La Barre, W. (1972) *The Ghost Dance*. New York: Delta.

Lefcourt, H. M. (1976) *Locus of Control: Current Trends in Theory and Research*. New York: John Wiley.

Lemert, E. M. (1972) *Human Deviation, Social Problems, and Social Control*, 2nd ed. Englewood Cliffs, NJ: Prentice-Hall.

Lerner, M. J., and Miller, D. T. (1978) Just world research and the attribution processes: Looking back and ahead. *Psychological Bulletin*, 85:1030-1051.

Lerner, M. J., Miller, D. T., and Holmes, J. G. (1976) Deserving and the emergence of forms of justice. In L. Berkowitz and E. Walster (Eds.),

Advances in Experimental Social Psychology (Vol. 9). New York: Academic Press.

Levine, F. (1974) *The Strange World of the Hare Krishnas*. New York: Fawcett.

Lieberman, M. A., Yalom, I. D., and Miles, M. B. (1973) *Encounter Groups: First Facts*. New York: Basic Books.

Lifton, R. J. (1961) *Thought Reform and the Psychology of Totalism: A Study of "Brainwashing" in China*. New York: Norton.

Lincoln, C. E. and Mamiya, L. H. (1980). Daddy Jones and Father Divine: The cult as a political religion. *Religion and Life*, 49:6-23.

Linville, P. W., and Jones, E. E. (1980) Polarized appraisals of out-group members. *Journal of Personality and Social Psychology*, 38:689-703.

Lofland, J. (1966) *Doomsday Cult: A Study of Conversion, Proselytization and Maintenance of Faith*. Englewood Cliffs, NJ: Prentice-Hall.

Lofland, J., and Stark, R. (1965) Becoming a world-saver: A theory of conversion to a deviant perspective. *American Sociological Review*, 30:862-875.

McGuire, W. J. (1967) Some impending reorientations in social psychology. *Journal of Experimental Social Psychology*, 3:124-139.

Mackenzie, K. D. (1978) *Organizational Structures*. Arlington Heights, IL.: AHM Publishing Corporation.

McLaughlin, B. (Ed.). (1969) *Studies in Social Movements: A Psychological Perspective*. New York: The Free Press.

Marcuse, H. (1964) *One-Dimensional Man*. Boston, MA: Beacon Press.

Marty, M. E. (1976) *Nation of Behavers*. Chicago: University of Chicago Press.

Mathison, R. R. (1960) *Faiths, Cults, and Sects in America*. New York: Bobbs-Merrill.

Matza, D. (1969) *Becoming Deviant*. Englewood Cliffs, NJ: Prentice-Hall.

Merton, R. K. (1957) *Social Theory and Social Structure*. Glencoe, IL: The Free Press.

Middlebrook, P. N. (1974) *Social Psychology and Modern Life*. New York: Alfred A. Knopf.

Milgram, S. (1974) *Obedience to Authority: An Experimental View*. New York: Harper & Row.

Miller, D. T., Norman, S. A., and Wright, E. (1978) Distortion in person perceptions as a consequence of the need for effective control. *Journal of Personality and Social Psychology*, 36:598-607.

Mischel, W. (1968) *Personality and Assessment*. New York: John Wiley.

— — —. (1977) On the future of personality measurement. *American Psychologist*, 32:246-254.

Morse, S., and Gergen, K. J. (1970) Social comparison, self-consistency and the concept of self. *Journal of Personality and Social Psychology*, 16:148-156.

Needleman, J., and Baker, G. (Eds.) (1978) *Understanding the New Religions*. New York: The Seabury Press.

Newcomb, T. M. (1943) *Personality and Social Change: Attitude Formation in a Student Community*. New York: Holt, Rinehart and Winston.

Newcomb, T. M., Koenig, K. E., Flacks, R., and Warwick, D. P. (1967) *Persistence and Change: Bennington College and Its Students after Twenty-five Years*. New York: John Wiley.

Nisbett, R. E., and Wilson, T. D. (1977) Telling more than we can know: Verbal reports on mental processes. *Psychological Review*, 84:231-259.

Paloutzian, R. F. (1976) Purpose-in-life and value changes following conversion. Paper presented at the meeting of the American Psychological Association, Washington, DC.

Paloutzian, R. F., Jackson, S. L., and Crandall, J. E. (1978) Conversion experience, belief systems, and personal and ethical attitudes. *Journal of Psychology and Theology*, 6:266-275.

Patrick, T., and Dulack, T. (1976) *Let Our Children Go*. New York: E. P. Dutton.

Pavlos, A. J. (1979) *Social Psychology and the Study of Deviant Behavior*. Washington, DC: University Press of America.

Penner, L. (1978) *Social Psychology: A Contemporary Approach*. New York: Oxford University Press.

Pepitone, A. (1976) Toward a normative and biocultural social psychology. *Journal of Personality and Social Psychology*, 34:641-653.

Perlman, E., and Havertat [pseud.] (Eds.) (1974) *Spiritual Community Guide for North America* (1975-1976). San Rafael, CA: Spiritual Community Publications.

Petersen, W. J. (1975) *Those Curious New Cults*. New Haven, CT: Keats.

Pliner, P., Heather, H., Kohl, J., and Saari, D. (1974) Compliance without pressure: Some further data on the foot-in-the-door technique. *Journal of Experimental Social Psychology*, 10:17-22.

Prabhupada, A.C.B. (1972) *Bahagavad-Gita As It Is*, abridged edition. New York: The Bhaktivedanta Book Trust.

Quarantelli, E. L., and Wenger, D. (1973) A voice from the 13th century: The characteristics and conditions for the emergence of a ouija board cult. *Urban Life and Culture*, 1:379-400.

Rice, B. (1976) Messiah from Korea: Honor Thy Father Moon. *Psychology Today*, 10:36-47.

Robbins, T., Anthony, D., Doucas, M., and Curtis, T. (1976) The last civil religion: The Unification Church of Reverend Sun Myung Moon. *Sociological Analysis*, 37:111-125.

Rokeach, M. (1973) *The Nature of Human Values*. New York: The Free Press.

Roof, W. C. (1978) Alienation and apostasy. *Society*, 15:41-45.

Rose, L. (1970) *Faith Healing*. Harmondsworth, Middlesex, England: Penguin Books Ltd.

Ross, L. (1977) The intuitive psychologist and his shortcomings: Distortions in the attribution process. In L. Berkowitz (Ed.), *Advances in Experimental Social Psychology* (Vol. 10) New York: Academic Press.

Roszak, T. (1969) *The Making of a Counter-Culture*. Garden City, NY: Doubleday.

Rothchild, J., and Wolf, S. B. (1976) *The Children of the Counterculture*. New York: Doubleday.

Salzman, L. (1966) Types of religious conversion. *Pastoral Psychology*, 17:8-20.

Sarnoff, I., and Zimbardo, P. G. (1961) Anxiety, fear, and social affiliation. *Journal of Abnormal and Social Psychology*, 62:356-363.

Schachter, S. (1964) The interaction of cognitive and physiological determinants of emotional state. In L. Berkowitz (Ed.), *Advances in Experimental Social Psychology* (Vol. 1). New York: Academic Press.

Schein, E. H., Schneider, I., and Baker, C. H. (1961) *Coercive Persuasion*. New York: Norton.

Schneider, D. J. (1976) *Social Psychology*. Reading, MA: Addison-Wesley.

Scobie, G.E.W. (1973) Types of Christian conversion. *Journal of Behavioral Science*, 1:265-271.

– – –. (1975) *Psychology of Religion*. New York: Halsted Press.

Scroggs, J. R., and Douglas, W.G.T. (1967) Issues in the psychology of religious conversion. *Journal of Religion and Health*, 6:204-216.

Sherif, M. (1936) *The Psychology of Social Norms*. New York: Harper.

Sherif, M., and Sherif, C. (1953) *Groups in Harmony and Tension*. New York: Harper.

Singer, M. T. (1979) Coming out of the cults. *Psychology Today*, 72:75-76, 79-80, 82.

Slade, M. (1979) New religious groups: Membership and legal battles. *Psychology Today*, 72:81.

Smith, A., Jr. (1978) Black reflections on the study of new religious consciousness. In J. Needleman and G. Baker (Eds.), *Understanding the New Religions*. New York: The Seabury Press, pp. 209-219.

Sneed, M. (1979) Brother Evangelist: hypnotic shepherd of a wandering ragtag flock. *The Chicago Tribune*, June 12.

Snyder, M., and Cunningham, M. R. (1975) To comply or not comply: Testing the self-perception explanation of the "foot-in-the-door" phenomenon. *Journal of Personality and Social Psychology*, 31:64-67.

Soderstrom, D. (1976) Religious orientation and meaning in life. *Psychologists Interested in Religious Issues Newsletter*, 1:4-10.

Sontag, F. (1977) *Sun Myung Moon*. Nashville, TN: Parthenon Press.

Stern, J. P. (1975) *Hitler: The Fuhrer and the People*. Berkeley: University of California Press.

Stogdill, R. M. (1974) *Handbook of Leadership: A Survey of Theory and Research*. New York: The Free Press.

Stoner, C., and Parke, J. A. (1978) *All Gods Children: The Cult Experience – Salvation or Slavery?* New York: Penguin Books.

Streiker, L. D. (1977) *The Cults Are Coming*. Nashville, TN: Abington.

Suedfeld, P. (1975) The benefits of boredom: Sensory deprivation reconsidered. *American Scientist*, 63:60-69.

Swope, G. W. (1980) Kids and cults: Who joins, and why. *Media and Methods*, 49:18-21.

Taylor, S. E., and Fiske, S. T. (1978) Salience, attention, and attribution: Top of the head phenomena. In L. Berkowitz (Ed.), *Advances in Experimental Social Psychology* (Vol. 11). New York: Academic Press.

Toch, H. (1965) *The Social Psychology of Social Movements*. Indianapolis, IN: Bobbs-Merrill.

Troeltsch, E. (1931) *The Social Teachings of the Christian Churches*. (O. Wyon, Trans.) New York: Macmillan.

Truax, C. B., and Cardhuff, R. R. (1967) *Toward Effective Counseling and Psychotherapy: Training and Practice*. Chicago: Aldine.

Tversky, A., and Kahneman, D. (1974) Judgment under uncertainty: Heuristics and biases. *Science*, 18:1124-1131.

Wallace, A.F.C. (1956) Revitalization movement. *American Anthropologist*, 58:264-281.

Wallace, R. K., and Benson, H. (1972) The physiology of meditation. *Scientific American*, 226:84-90.

Walster, E. (1966) Assignment of responsibility for an accident. *Journal of Personality and Social Psychology*, 3:73-79.

Washington, J.R., Jr. (1972) *Black Sects and Cults*. New York: Doubleday.

Weber, M. (1947) *Theory of Social and Economic Organization*. New York: The Free Press.

— — —. (1961). The routinization of charisma. In T. Parsons, K. D. Naegeel, and J. R. Pitts (Eds.), *Theories of Society*. New York: The Free Press.

— — —. (1963) *The Sociology of Religion*. Boston, MA: Beacon Press.

West, S. G., Gum, S. P., and Chernicky, P. (1975) Ubiquitous Watergate: An attributional analysis. *Journal of Personality and Social Psychology*, 32:55-65.

Wicklund, R. A., and Brehm, J. W. (1976) *Perspectives on Cognitive Dissonance*. New York: Halsted Press.

Wilson, B. R. (1969) The Pentecostalist minister: Role conflicts and status contradictions. In B. McLaughlin (Ed.), *Studies in Social Movements*. New York: The Free Press, pp. 444-460.

Wilson, D. W., and Schafer, R. P. (1978) Is social psychology interdisciplinary? *Personality and Social Psychology Bulletin*, 4:548-552.

Windemiller, D. A. (1960) The psychodynamics of change in religious conversion and communist brainwashing: With particular reference to the 18th-century Evangelical revival and the Chinese thought control movement. Unpublished doctoral dissertation, Boston University.

Worsley, P. M. (1959) Cargo cults. *Scientific American*, 200:126-128.

Wortman, C. B., and Silver, R. (1980) Coping with undesirable life events. In M.E.P. Seligman and J. Garber (Eds.), *Human Helplessness: Theory and Applications*. New York: Academic Press.

Wuthnow, R. and Glock, C. Y. (1973) Religious loyalty, defection, and experimentation among college youth. *Journal for the Scientific Study of Religion*, 12:157-180.

Yablonsky, L. (1967) *Synanon: The Tunnel Back*. Baltimore, MD: Penguin Books.

Yankelovich, D. (1974) *The New Morality: A Profile of American Youth in the 70's*. New York: McGraw-Hill.

Yinger, J. M. (1970) *The Scientific Study of Religion*. New York: Macmillan.

Zablocki, B. (1971) *The Joyful Community*. Baltimore, MD: Penguin.

Zald, M. N., and Ash, R. (1966) Social movement organization: Growth, decay, and change. *Social Forces*, 44:327-341.

Zimbardo, P. G., Ebbesen, E. G., and Maslach, C. (1977) *Influencing Attitudes and Changing Behavior*, 2nd ed. Reading, MA: Addison-Wesley.

Index

About the Author

ANDREW JOHN PAVLOS is Professor of Psychology at George Williams College in Downers Grove, Illinois. He is also the author of *Social Psychology and the Study of Deviant Behavior*.